the
**GARLIC
FARM
SHOP**

Credits

This book was made by:

Editor
Natasha Edwards

Recipes
Columbine Mulvey
Charlie Bartlett
Jenny Boswell
Josephine Boswell
Paddy Bradshaw

Contributions
Colin Boswell
Alexa Boswell
Barbara Muston

Design and Illustration
Paul Scott Mulvey

Typography by MatreroG

Photography
Paul Scott Mulvey
Tim Hatcher
Heather Edwards

Artwork
Ben Davey

Published by
The Garlic Press

Printed on 100% recycled
paper using vegetable
based inks

Contents

INTRODUCTION

The Garlic Farm is all about garlic

The history, mystery and magic of this plant has intrigued and seduced people from all over the world for hundreds of generations. The Boswell family first grew garlic in the late seventies when Colin planted his first crop. The Garlic Farm has grown, bulb by bulb, and now produces over twenty garlic varieties, countless tasty products and has a popular Garlic Farm Shop and restaurant which are visited and enjoyed by many. The family, the farm team and our customers continue to be entranced by garlic: one of nature's most powerful culinary gifts.

There's no doubt that Colin is in thrall to garlic's magical power. He's developed a deep passion for it spending years in the field, glasshouse and study accumulating knowledge and developing new garlic varieties for growing in the UK. He's travelled to the foothills of the Tien Shan mountains in Kazakhstan, to deepest Turkey and the Caucasus in search of the original garlic plant, or as he likes to call it 'the mother of all garlic'. But that's another book in the making...

Growing garlic for many years on the Isle of Wight, we've gathered not only some great recipes but a huge range of garlic information. This book is our way of sharing our garlic knowledge with you and we hope it will bring flavour to your tables, health to your heart, love in your garden... and fewer blood sucking friends.

Natasha (Boswell) Edwards, Editor

Martin and Norah Boswell 1951

Colin Boswell and family 1982

Colin & Martin Boswell 1984

THE GARLIC FARM STORY

We've come a long way since the 1950s when my grandparents, Martin and Norah Boswell, arrived on the Isle of Wight in search of suitable land to fulfil their dreams of a farming life. From a 140 acre mixed tenant farm to the UK's only specialist garlic grower, Colin Boswell (Dad), the garlic farmer tells the story...

My father, Martin, started farming on 10 acres on the North Downs in Kent in the late 1940s. I was born there in 1952 and remember it well. We had cows, pigs and hens and by the time we left in 1957, he was farming 50 acres.

We moved to the Isle of Wight because at that time, land was cheaper here and, importantly for a young farmer seeking wider acres, there were farms to take on as a tenant.

There were over 100 applicants for Mersley Farm. Martin impressed the agents who made all the decisions on behalf of the owners, the Carter estate, by going over to their Southampton office with a plan on how he proposed to farm the 140 acres.

We had a dairy herd, pigs and numerous different intensive cash crops which were trialled every year, including watercress, chicory, runner beans, asparagus and sweet corn. The island climate produced good sweet corn and in the early 60s UK consumers were just beginning to experiment, moving away from their traditional mundane food offering which was not significantly different from what had been available in 1860.

Martin was the first large producer of sweet corn in the UK and, through the 60s and 70s, the business flourished, selling to the growing supermarket chains and in the still vibrant wholesale fruit and vegetable markets across the UK.

Colin in Kazakhstan in search of the Mother of all Garlic 2008

Selling corn at The Isle of Wight Pop Festival 1970

Colin with a bumper Garlic harvest 1990

The first Garlic Festival Queen 1984

Mersley Farm was purchased from the landlords in 1963, followed by the acquisition of two more neighbouring farms. By 1976, the farm extended to 320 acres but the dairy herd had gone, replaced by 100 acres of sweet corn.

By 1976 I had spent three years in market research and advertising in London and Kent, experience that proved invaluable later on, but I wanted to free myself and my future wife Jenny by farming on our own account in the Isle of Wight on the family farm, where prospects looked enticing. Jenny and I met at Nottingham University where she studied Russian and I economics.

The summers of 1975 and 1976 will be remembered by all who lived through them as very hot and dry. My mother Norah grew some garlic in the kitchen garden in 1975, producing beautiful white, glistening bulbs, unlike the typical offering on the supermarket shelves.

We needed to get another crop into production to expand the business and the sums on garlic looked promising. One looked at the price on the supermarket shelf, estimated what the supermarket might have paid for it and then multiplied that figure by another estimate of what might be produced from one acre on the farm.

Any grower will tell you that it doesn't quite work out like that but, at the age of 24, hope springs eternal and I began to study every aspect of garlic production. My O level French improved remarkably – it had to - and with visits to France and California, I was learning more each year. As a result, in 1979, we were able to break into Tesco followed by Sainsbury, Marks and Spencer and Safeway.

We quickly found that, from our own Isle of Wight production, we could supply only a small fraction of the garlic required for what amounted eventually to 70% of the UK garlic market, so we imported from growers in Spain, California, South America and Hungary.

The Boswell Family at the Garlic Festival 2006

The Garlic Farm Team 2010

Marks and Spencer insisted that fresh garlic be used in all their new recipe dishes which boomed in the 80s and 90s. The British discovered a love affair with Garlic Bread and Chicken Kiev. It was estimated that this "passive" garlic consumption meant that the British were consuming more garlic in southeast England than in Northern France.

We became the major supplier of peeled garlic and garlic purée to M&S food manufacturers and others, producing 20 tonnes a week in these lines alone.

The business grew fast through the 1980s and, by 1995, employed 300 people in the summer, 120 all year round. The large supermarkets came to dominate the scene and to dictate the life and values of those who supplied them.

In 1999 we sold the business that supplied the supermarkets and returned to our roots as growers of our own quality garlic, selling direct in farmers' markets and to the fast growing farm retail sector, which is now the fastest growing part of the UK fresh retail market.

Our five children, Oliver, Natasha, Hugo, Josephine and Alexa, all became well known faces at farmers' markets in London and Hampshire and at shows and food festivals across the UK. We created the concept of "The Garlic Farm on the Isle of Wight", which was boosted by a continual stream of television coverage owing to the unique situation we are in as the UK's largest specialist garlic grower.

From over 30 years of garlic growing, we have selected strains of garlic that grow well in the UK and market them to amateur gardeners, both direct and through all the major garden seed companies. Pick up almost any seed catalogue and you will see that the majority of garlic on offer ends in "Wight". These are all supplied by us, proven to grow well in the UK and increasingly popular, as more households discover the pleasure and satisfaction of growing their own vegetables and garlic.

To provide background and a wider knowledge base to everything we do, I travel widely to research the origins of garlic. So far this quest has taken me to Kazakhstan's Tien Shan region, searching for the Mother of all Garlic from which all garlic strains are descended; eastern Turkey on the Iran/Iraq border; Georgia and the Caucasus.

Our shop at Mersley Farm began as our own farm retail outlet in 2000, expanding every year to the point where we now have alongside an acclaimed restaurant, farm walks and demonstrations of garlic growing – our own garlic centre.

LAUTREC WIGHT

PROVENCE WIGHT

VENETIAN WIGHT

PURPLE WIGHT

PICARDY WIGHT

SOLENT WIGHT

GARLIC VARIETIES

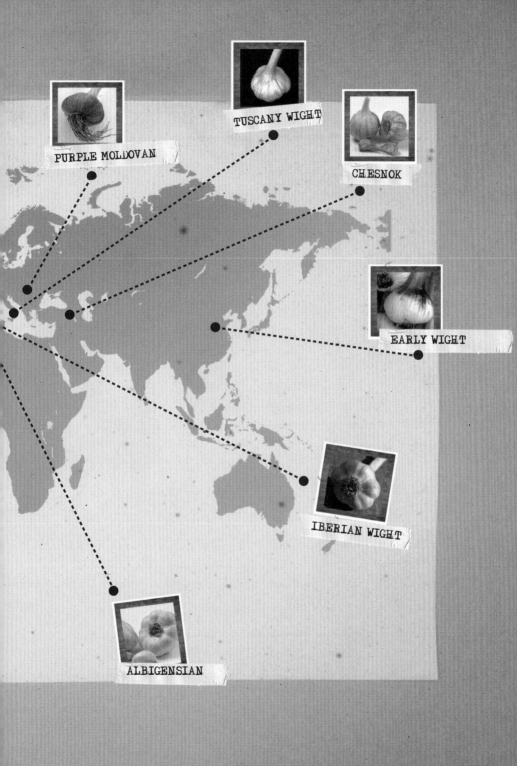

PURPLE MOLDOVAN

TUSCANY WIGHT

CHESNOK

EARLY WIGHT

IBERIAN WIGHT

ALBIGENSIAN

GARLIC VARIETIES EXPLAINED

Garlic divides into two distinct types: hardnecks (ophioscorodon) and softnecks (sativum). Hardnecks are generally more winter hardy and closer in evolution to their origins in the mountains of Central Asia.

Hardneck varieties

All hardneck garlic produce a flowering stalk which is the "hardneck". Snap this off as soon as it appears and use in stirfries. The result will be, in some cases, a doubling of the size of the bulb.

Purple Moldovan

June harvest, with dark green broad vigorous leaf growth. Produces 5-6 large fat cloves around a central core. Probable origin in allium longicuspis from Kazahkstan. Easy to use due to large clove size. A warm garlic with real persistence and amazing aroma. Makes the best garlic bread.
Keeps until Christmas.

Chesnok Wight

June harvest, white skinned bulbs with rich black veins on the outside and 6-10 purple cloves inside. More productive type than Moldovan. Origin in the Ukraine, around Kiev. Keeps until January. Spicy heat close to Moldovan intensity.

Lautrec Wight

Harvest in June. White skinned, pink cloved, from near Toulouse, SW France. The most versatile of hardnecks, can be planted autumn or early spring but dislikes wet conditions. Better for south of England. Held by French gourmands to be the best tasting of all French garlic. Keeps until February.

Aquila Wight

Red, early hardneck garlic from the Appenine town of Aquila, near Rome in the Abruzzo region. Plant October for harvest end May/early June. Sold widely as green early garlic and made into a paste with olive oil called "crastatelli". Will keep until November.

Red Sicilian

Another red hardneck, also known as Nubian Red, this is similar to Aquila but warmer and spicier. Very popular in Sicily in traditional dishes and roasted on barbecues. Plant October and harvest beginning June.

Softneck varieties

Venetian Wight

Harvest in July. A beautiful white garlic from the Po Valley in Italy. Very close to Solent Wight. Small, hard white garlic with high density and a good keeper. Best planted in December/January.

GARLIC for
PLANTING

£2 each or
3 bulbs for £5

Make your selection
label the bag with the
variety chosen
full growing instructions

Venetian Wight

Plant Early Spring. Keeps
to March year after harvest,
exposes rich-red flavour,
similar to Solent Wight, a
softneck from the Po Valley
in Italy.

Chesnok Wight
Allium Sativum Ophioscorodon

One of many beautiful and fiery
Eastern European hardneck garlic.
This one comes from the Ukraine.

Plant in autumn, harvest in July and
it will keep till September.

Lautrec Wight
Allium sativum ophioscorodon

From the village of Lautrec, near
Toulouse, considered by many to
be France's finest garlic.

A hardneck with a white outer skin
and large pink even cloves inside.
Plant in autumn or early spring,
snapping off and eating the
"rocambole" flowering twirl. Does

Provence Wight
Allium Sativum

A large, white softneck garlic typical
of those found in the markets every-
where in Provence. This garlic will
mature two weeks after Iberian Wight,
towards the end of June. Large fat
cloves ideal in the vegetable and fish
dishes of the Mediterranean, this will
keep until January.

Unlike many Mediterranean
this should grow

Iberian Wight
Allium Sativum

A large white softneck garlic,
purple when grown close to
surface, originating around
Cordoba in SW Spain.

The earliest quality white garlic,
performing well in the

Albigensian Wight
Allium Sativum

A large white softneck garlic
with purple hints from the
land of the 13th century
heretic Cathars in SW France

Exceptional size & quality from
autumn to early spring plantings.

Elephant Garlic
Allium Ampeloprasum

Elephant Garlic, not a true garlic, but a
leek with a gentle garlic aroma. Bulbs
grow up to 10 inches/25cm across with
a beautiful flower.

It grows wild throughout Euro
isolated outcrops around

Solent Wight
Allium Sativum

Solent Wight, the original Isle of Wight
garlic, particularly suited to our UK
climate.

Originating from the aristocrats of late
garlic types – Venetian, Hungarian and
Auvergne, it is the longest keeping,
until April, and has superb length and
strength of flavour with real "bouquet".

The best for late green garlic and when
dry, for plaiting.

Plant in Autumn or Spring as late as
March. Best results from January/
February planting.

Any 3 Bulbs for £5

Early Purple Wight
Harvest end May, beginning June. Large purple bulbs with very wide leafy growth. The first taste of new season garlic, en primeur. Dries very quickly and usually consumed green. Purple garlic with origins in China. Best consumed within 3 months after harvest. Keeps until October but no longer.

Mediterranean Wight
Harvest in mid-June. Large, early, white flat garlic, typical of the Mediterranean region but grows well in the UK. Rewarding to grow, vigorous and leafy. Fat juicy cloves excellent for aioli and bouillabaisse. Keeps until January.

Iberian Wight
Ready in June, two weeks before Albigensian. Large flat white garlic with purple stripes, origin in south west Spain. Plant it at least 60mm deep as it tends to push up and grow on top of the ground. Excellent all round garlic with large cloves. Keeps until January.

Albigensian Wight
Late June harvest. Large white garlic with deep rather than flat bulb. Can be planted as late as January as well as in autumn. Origin in Southwest France. The garlic of the 13th century, heretical Cathars, known to Da Vinci Code and Holy Grail followers. Plant a little heresy in your garden. Keeps until February, longer than other Mediterranean softnecks.

Solent Wight
Mid-July harvest. January or February planting is best. This is our most robust garlic in terms of overall eating and keeping quality. Large, hard, dense, white bulbs with an elegant bouquet. Retains flavour during cooking. Easiest garlic to plait and will keep well until at least April.

Picardy Wight
Originating in the fields of Picardy, growing on the battlefields of the Somme and the surrounding area. Adapted to cooler and wetter conditions, will grow anywhere in the UK that has proved a challenge to other garlic. In its native region it is plaited and smoked due to its longevity. Harvested after mid July it will keep to May the following year. Best planted in December/January

Tuscany Wight
Harvest in July. A new spring planted softneck from Tuscany. Good keeping quality and most significant of all, big fat cloves all the way through the bulb. May prove in future to be the most popular garlic we sell. Best planted in December and January.

Elephant Garlic
Harvested green in June, it will be dry by mid July. A fun member of the allium family, Elephant Garlic can grow, with adequate water, to 15 cm across and weigh over a kilo. It has a warm mild garlic flavour but is increasingly popular with those who like to make a statement in their cooking. For best results plant September/October.

GROWING YOUR OWN
GARLIC

There's something naturally satisfying about growing and harvesting your own produce and, we would argue, none more so than garlic. From planting to harvest takes up to nine months and when the beautiful white heads are teased from mother earth you'll feel pride like a new parent. At the Garlic Farm, when the first bulbs are brought into the farmyard there is a real buzz of excitement and lots of cooing at their beauty. They take on tastier and more attractive proportions each year... well, we might be kidding ourselves there but we like to think they just get better and better. Garlic growers the world over, from those with a few pots on the patio to many acres, share each year this same sensation of wonderment at nature's bounty.

Here are our best tips on how to grow fantastic garlic.

When to plant

The timing of garlic planting will largely depend on the variety you are growing. As a general rule, planting earlier in the autumn or the spring, according to type, will give you better results.

Planting times are important; garlic needs certain conditions of light, temperature and moisture in order to reproduce and swell. If you plant late, you're likely to be disappointed.

Autumn Planting Garlic Types

Plant September to December.

Hard necks: Purple Heritage Moldovan, Lautrec Wight, Aquila Wight and Chesnok Wight, Elephant Garlic.
Softnecks: Early Purple Wight, Albigensian Wight, Provence Wight, Iberian Wight, Mediterranean Wight.

Spring Planting Garlic Types

Plant December to April.

Hard necks: Lautrec Wight (up until February)
Soft necks: Solent Wight, Tuscany Wight, Venetian Wight (up until March), Picardy Wight (up until April)

Preparing the ground for garlic

Garlic loves the sun, so choose the sunniest position possible to get the best results. It will still grow in the shade though so don't despair if you're out of sunny spots in the veg patch. Try to choose a part of the vegetable garden that has not had members of the onion family (leeks, onions, spring onions, chives, garlic) on it for two years to reduce the risk of disease.

For a good crop, good soil is important. You can work with whatever soil you have in your garden by adding extra nutritive ingredients to make it more garlic friendly. As with all other garden plants, well-draining but moisture retaining soil and a neutral to slightly acidic pH is ideal.

Garlic does not do well with any over supply of nitrogen in our UK climate. In hotter, drier locations, garlic can use more nitrogen but in our damp climate, too much nitrogen will produce split bulbs, soft cloves and reduce the life of the bulbs once dried by at least a half. But the addition of some good compost before planting can avoid the classic symptoms of yellowing, poor vigour and small sized bulbs.

Most garden soils have goodsupplies of phosphate and potash from over-zealous fertilising by their occupants. Garlic needs some phosphate but more importantly needs sulphate of potash. If you want to invest in any fertiliser for your garlic, buy some sulphate of potash to be applied in February.

Dig and turn over your soil to the depth of your spade at least and deeper, provided you are turning up good topsoil and not lighter coloured subsoil. Add sandy gravel to heavy clay soil to improve drainage and add lime to acidic soil. Work it down so that you have a fine tilth of at least 4 cm (2").

Planting the cloves

When you're ready to plant, and not before, break up the bulb into individual cloves, taking care not to damage them. The cloves must be planted, root down, pointed end up, deep enough so that they can be covered with 3 to 4 cm (1 ½" to 2") of loose soil (measured from the point). You can plant them individually, in small holes or draw out a furrow, 3 to 4 cm deep and place your cloves just resting in the soil at the bottom of the furrow, with half the clove exposed. Spacing should be 15 cm (6") apart for large cloves and 10 cm (4") apart for small cloves (the ones from the centre of the bulb). When the whole row is planted, draw the soil over the cloves to cover them completely.

If you don't have enough space in your vegetable garden, or even your flower borders, you can plant your garlic in large containers or pots; allow 4 cloves per 15cm (6") pot.

Tending your garlic crop

Up to two months after planting, you will see the green shoot of each clove emerging, marking the rows. Autumn planting is slower to emerge than spring.

In February sprinkle Sulphate of Potash at a rate of 3oz per square yard (100g per square metre), around your emerging plants and lightly hoe or fork it in.

All you need to do then is keep your garlic plants weed-free and never let them dry out. If you want good sized bulbs, water them and keep watering them from March onwards until a week before harvest. Keep the soil moist. Cease watering one week before harvest to aid the transition from growth to storage.

Garlic's wild habitat is on mountain slopes, emerging just below the snow line in March, and watered by a constant trickle of melting snow through its roots. The life cycle of garlic has evolved around the availability of this melting snow water, from March until June. As the water diminishes in June, so bulb growth ceases and senescence begins. The bulb dries and goes to sleep until reawakened by its physiological clock in response to winter cold followed by warmer moist conditions the following spring.

Scapes and Rocamboles

Scapes and Rocamboles are the flowering heads of hardneck garlic types.

"Scape" is the generic name for all hardneck garlic flowering heads but some types have a tendency for the stem to twist and curl, sometimes as many as three to four times, and these are called "Rocamboles". We will refer to them all here as scapes.

In June and July you will notice a pointed bud pushing out from the centre of each of your hardneck garlic plants. This bud will emerge in a matter of days and within a week of first appearing, it will be held on a stem above the leaf canopy of the plant.

If you want to maximise your bulb size, snap the scape off just above the leaves and use it in a stir fry - it's delicious. Removing the scape the moment it appears can increase bulb size by as much as 50%. The plant's energy for reproduction is then focussed on its only alternative, the bulb.

If you leave the scape, the bud will eventually burst open into a purple flowerhead of tiny flowers and sometimes tiny garlic cloves. The flowers will not produce viable seed though the tiny cloves can be used to grow more garlic, like the cloves in the bulb, but the results are unreliable and may take several years.

Our advice is to snap off the scape at first sight, eat it and enjoy it and, when you come to harvest, enjoy lifting a larger bulb rather than a meagre one that has had to compete for nourishment with the flowering head above ground.

Harvest

For softneck varieties, the best time to harvest your garlic is when half the crop stems have completely drooped to one side. For hardnecks, the best time is when about 30% of the leaves have started to go brown. These signs mean the bulbs are completely matured. This is the really exciting bit. Lift your garlic carefully from the soil and brush off the excess dirt before laying it in a tray. It is then best to dry it in the sunniest, driest place available. If the weather is very dry and hot, then the bulbs can be laid out in the garden but it's probably best if they are put in a glass house or under cover to dry. You'll know when the garlic is completely dry because there will be no greenness left in the stem and the outer layers of skin will brush off easily. This can take a few weeks. Of course, you can still use the garlic before it has completely dried or even when it is still quite green (see our green garlic recipes for ideas). Remember to keep the stems on if you intend to plait or grappe your garlic for storage.

Storage

The best place to store garlic is a dry, warmish environment. Hanging up in the kitchen is fine. Never put your garlic in the fridge; the cold and dark will encourage it to sprout. The most convenient and beautiful way of storing garlic is to make it into a plait or grappe which can be hung in your kitchen. It adds character to your kitchen and helps the garlic keep for longer.

HOW TO PLAIT GARLIC

Strong hands and patience required

All the Boswell children have spent at least a few summers sitting out in the sun cleaning and plaiting garlic to earn some pocket money. We've created quite competitive, exacting standards for our plaits - any slackness or floppy bulbs will just not do. For the novice though, you should be able to make a decent looking plait if you've got a pair of strong hands and some patience.

To make a plait you will need at least ten good sized garlic bulbs with the stems on. You can clean them first by using your thumb to brush off the outer layers of skin then use some secateurs to trim the roots. Be careful not to cut the actual flesh of the garlic (or your fingers).

1. Arrange the bulbs in pairs of similar size.

2. Start with the two largest bulbs. These will form the base of the plait. To begin, wrap the stem of one bulb very tightly around the other as close to the bulbs of each as possible.

3. Holding the two bulbs in place, take another bulb from the next smallest pair and place it at the centre. Take the protruding stem and wrap it over the base of the stem from the bulb just added.

4. Take the fourth bulb and place it next to its pair then hold it in place by wrapping the stem to the left into the middle (you're starting to plait now)

5. Continue to add bulbs in this fashion being careful always to pull the plait as tight as possible as you add each one. When all the bulbs are added, continue to plait the stems for a few centimetres then finish off with some raffia or garden string, make a loop for hanging then use secateurs to trim off any stray bits of stem or roots.

Voila! Beautiful.

HOW TO GRAPPE GARLIC

The easier way to display your garlic

This is the slightly easier option for displaying your garlic.

Making garlic into grappes (small bunches) can be easily done with any number or size of bulbs. It's best done with good quality raffia but you could also use garden string.

1. Take a good metre and a half of raffia or string.

2. Take the largest bulb and wrap the raffia around the stem as close to the bulb as possible, tying it at one end.

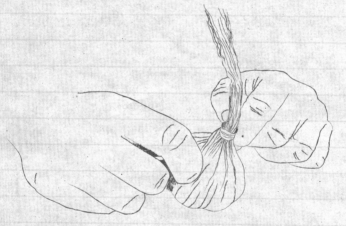

3. Take another bulb and place it next to the first one then wrap the raffia around the stem, close to the bulb then around both the stems a couple of times, pulling them tightly together. You should be able to make it quite tight without breaking the stem, but don't be too keen.

4. Continue to add bulbs, wrapping first around the stem added, then around all the stems until you have what looks like a posy of garlic.

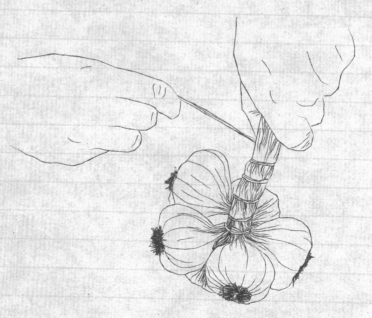

5. Once you have added an adequate number of bulbs (we usually find 6-9 looks best,) continue to wrap the raffia tightly around the stems in a spiral for about 12 cm then finish off and make a loop with the raffia for hanging.

THE GARLIC YEAR

The Garlic Year has to start with planting and the earliest garlic wants to be in the ground in September.

September
Anytime in September plant Elephant Garlic for the biggest result, also Early Wight and Early Purple Garlic. Clear the area for garlic planting. If not too dry, dig, otherwise wait for some rain. Work in some general fertiliser. Apply very well rotted dung in moderation.

Elephant Garlic. Early Garlic Varieties – Early Purple Wight, Early Wight.

October-November
Plant all the Autumn types in these two months, earlier the better.

**Softnecks - Iberian, Albigensian, Mediterranean, Provence
Hardnecks – Purple Moldovan, Chesnok.**

December
Still time to plant Autumn types and plant some Spring types after Christmas.

Lautrec will do well from a December planting.

January
Spring garlic planting, seize any opportunity that nature gives to plant Spring types.

Solent Wight, Tuscany Wight, Picardy Wight. Also plant Lautrec but a little late for other hardnecks.

February
Continue spring planting as weather allows. Provided the garlic is now marking the rows and about 10cm tall, apply Sulphate of Potash at 100g per square metre. You could also work in dried blood or a light dressing of nitrogen - but don't overdo it.

March
Early March plantings can give good results of the spring garlic types. From now on, bulbs get smaller if planted late. Keep top dressing with Sulphate of Potash if not already applied in February and small additional amounts of nitrogen fertiliser. Keep the ground clear of weeds by hoeing. Vital that the soil is well aerated but be careful not to break the garlic's roots.

April
Very last time for planting Spring garlic but do not expect large bulbs.

Continue hoeing and aerating the soil.

Vital that the garlic is watered if dry. Now is the time that the plant decides if it is short of water and so prepares to grow a smaller bulb according to the resources available. By the end of April you should have applied at least one application of rust preventative such as Dithane. You could also apply sulphur as a liquid to give some protection.

May
Weeding and watering are the order of the day. Continue rust protection every 10 days.

Start harvesting your first green garlic at the end of the month.

June
Look out for flowering spikes on Elephant Garlic and scapes on hardnecks. Snap them off as they appear. Bulb size will double. Keep watering all but Early Wight until the middle of June and Spring garlic types until the end of June. Ruthlessly suppress weed growth. Early Wight will be ready to harvest by the first week in June in the South, later in the North. If the weather is dry leave the harvested bulbs with their leaves on in the sun to dry. If wet, then replicate a Mediterranean summer under cover of glass or plastic.

Early Wight ready to lift. Elephant Garlic can be harvested as green garlic from the beginning of the month and harvested as dry garlic by the end. Iberian, Provence, Albigensian and Mediterranean will be ready as green garlic by the middle of June and can be harvested as their leaves lie on the ground by the end of June. For the best quality and colour, harvest early.

July
Continue to dry the June harvest. Early Wight will be dry within a week but others will take longer. Remember it stores better with its leaves on. Start harvesting Solent Wight in the middle of July. If the stems start to lie on the ground it is time to lift. Don't leave it too late.

August
Take bunches of garlic out of direct sunlight. It is dry when there is no more moisture in the neck. Try plaiting and grapping.

Make presents to your friends of your own plaited garlic. Study seed catalogues and visit www.thegarlicfarm.co.uk to decide which types to plant this year. Order your autumn garlic in good time.

GARLIC'S MAGICAL FLAVOUR FACTORY

Time for a little chemistry

One of the most exciting things about garlic as an ingredient is that its taste can vary dramatically depending on how it is prepared. Crushing versus cooking whole, you may have noticed, produces very different flavours. This is all thanks to the chemical composition of garlic. At the same time, the preparation of garlic will affect its therapeutic benefits.

Three components of garlic affect its taste and therapeutic properties: Allicin, alliin and allinase. The sulphur compound allicin is responsible for the flavour, smell and to a great extent, the medicinal effects of garlic. Yet, strangely, there is no allicin present in a whole clove.. haha, completely foxed? Well, allicin is only created when the enzyme of allinase interacts with the alliin, both present in separate cells of the clove. When the two are combined, allicin is created. So, when you chop, crush, press, or bite into garlic, a fantastic chemical reaction is taking place, creating allicin. Hence, the odourless whole clove miraculously and almost immediately turns into one of the most arresting taste and aroma experiences of the natural world.

When allinase and alliin interact, this produces not only allicin but lots of other sulphur compounds which contribute to taste and health properties. In general, if garlic is cooked whole, it will not only be milder but also much simpler in composition and very different from garlic that has been chopped or crushed prior to cooking.

So, knowing this about garlic helps to give an indication of how we should prepare garlic for different taste effects. Here we'll cover the most common preparations. We'll explain the health benefits of garlic later but always bear in mind that the medicinal properties of garlic are best when the garlic is crushed (creating allicin) and raw... this may not be the most preferable way to eat it if you're worried about lingering garlic breath but it really is the only way to get all the best therapeutic effects.

Although garlic is used raw in some dishes, the classic continental culinary approach is to mince or crush garlic before sautéing it until soft and coloured before adding other liquids. This provides that rich and delicious foundation to your dish, but the allicin in crushed raw garlic is destroyed by heat. If you want to retain the aromatic, vivid and more aggressive garlic taste, you should add crushed garlic towards the end of the cooking. The recipes in this book explore many different ways of preparing garlic, resulting in a wide range of flavours and textures - all with their own merit. Here we tell you some of the techniques for preparing and cooking garlic.

Peeling

Garlic getting under your fingernails? We like the lingering smell of garlic when you've been cooking but admit it's not always desirable. Peeling can be a bit of a chore until you get a knack that suits you. Don't let the peeling hold back your garlic consumption! It's all part of the process. Here are some tips. If you buy good quality, large bulbs with large cloves then immediately this job is made easier. You'll find the older and drier the bulb, the easier it is to peel. Solent Wight bulbs usually have lovely large cloves and the skin falls off quite easily once you get started. If you intend to crush or press the cloves, you can use the flat side of a knife to crush the clove slightly onto a chopping board, causing the skins to naturally break away. If you use a lot of garlic or intend the entire clove to remain intact, the little garlic peeling tube is a handy way for a quick peel and means no garlic under the fingernails.

Crushing

Crushing garlic with a garlic press or with a pestle and mortar gives the most pungent taste. By completely breaking down all the cells within the clove, creating the maximum reaction of allinase with the sulphur compounds, we can fully explore the potential complexity of flavour of the garlic. Crushed garlic is not only the best way to get a strong flavour but also gives the best health benefits, provided it is not cooked. Heat and acid will inactivate the enzyme allinase which helps create allicin.

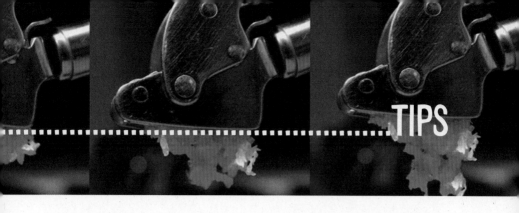

So if you are adding crushed garlic to vinegar for a vinaigrette for example, it's best not to crush the garlic directly into the vinegar or lemon juice, but wait for a few seconds while the chemical reaction takes place before adding it.Cooking will destroy allicin but if you chop or crush garlic before heating it, many other compounds will be created which will create their own flavour and likely additional health benefits.

Chopping, Slicing and Mincing
If you're frying your garlic in oil or adding it to a stir fry then these methods can work well to give that rich, sweet and nutty flavour. By chopping, the chemical reaction in the garlic is not activated fully so will give a milder flavour than crushing. Sliced garlic can give a good visual effect if you're adding it to sautéed vegetables or in a salad. Lightly salting the garlic can also enhance its flavour. Whatever you do though, don't cook the garlic until it is anywhere near dark brown or burn it as the flavour will then be quite unpleasant. We've all done it once and it's not good.

Cooking garlic whole and roasting garlic
When garlic is cooked as whole cloves, no chemical reaction takes place to create allicin or other sulphur compounds so the flavour of the clove will be very much milder and quite different to crushed garlic. Roasting garlic with skins intact gives a wonderful mild, sweet, caramelized taste which is very popular. Again, no aromatic flavour compounds are produced but the effect is visually brilliant and tastes delicious.

THE SEASONS
SPRING

Recipes for spring

When the sun is low in the sky, the ground is still wet enough for wellies, the green shoots of the garlic crop are starting to make their first hesitant appearance and the asparagus tips are miraculously springing out of the wet earth overnight, we're mostly found chasing off bands of hungry rabbits trying to destroy the fruits of our labours. They're lucky if they get away though as they're most likely to end up in the pot.There's a wonderful quality to the light in spring that brings glistening freshness to the colours of the valley. It's the perfect time for walks along uncrowded Isle of Wight beaches and downs. Spring comes early to the Island and we're always very proud to announce the very first harvest of asparagus in the UK. Also available are early Isle of Wight potatoes and tomatoes, succulent Island lamb, purple sprouting broccoli and of course, our own green garlic. The key to all this season's produce is in its freshness. Recipes in this section are inspired by fresh springtime ingredients from the Isle of Wight.

- Green garlic pesto
- Charlie's asparagus, garlic and chilli changa
- Jenny's roast lamb fillet
- Roasted purple-sprouting broccoli
- Garlic Farm ciabatta
- Roasted elephant garlic soup
- Happy chicken with loads of cloves
- Prawn and pak choi stir fry
- Rabbit, pancetta and wild garlic risotto

GREEN GARLIC PESTO

Green garlic is available from April to May. The bulbs are harvested before they have reached full maturity and started to dry and so the flavour is milder and fresher and the flesh is juicier. If you can't wait for the garlic harvest in July, this is a perfect way to enjoy an early crop. You can use it simply stirred into fresh pasta, spread onto meats before cooking, on toast, in a salad dressing...you decide.

> 3 large bulbs green garlic, untrimmed (leave all the green stems on, you'll use these too)
> 4 tablespoons of extra virgin olive oil
> 1/2 teaspoon sea salt
> 4 tablespoons of toasted pine nuts, sunflower seeds and pumpkin seeds
> A good handful of fresh basil leaves
> 150g of grated pecorino or parmesan cheese

Trim and discard the roots of green garlic, finely chop (including stems). Place all ingredients in a blender or food processor (or using pestle and mortar if you prefer a chunkier texture), pulse until smooth or to the desired consistency. Add more salt to taste and stir in more olive oil if too dry. This pesto keeps very well, covered and chilled up to 3 days or frozen up to 2 months.

"green garlic is milder in flavour and the flesh juicier"

CHARLIE'S ASPARAGUS, GARLIC AND CHILLI CHANGA

"a unique way to show off Isle of Wight asparagus"

This is a Garlic Farm restaurant signature dish and is a feisty, unique and delicious way to show off succulent Isle of Wight asparagus. Charlie developed this with a bit of inspiration from Colin, having just returned from a trip to Turkey. The poached eggs are best served very runny.

Serves 2 as main, 4 as starter

A good sized bunch of thick Isle of Wight asparagus spears
4 eggs, cracked into ramekins
Egg cup of white wine vinegar (for poaching)
1/3 packet of butter, melted
1 chopped red chilli
4 tablespoons of thick Greek yoghurt
2 cloves Solent Wight garlic, finely chopped

Bring two saucepans of water to the boil, one slightly salted, for the asparagus and the other with the white wine vinegar to make perfect poached eggs. Add the asparagus to the salted water and cook until tender (about 7 minutes). Meanwhile, mix the melted butter with the chopped chilli and mix the garlic into the thick yoghurt. When the water with the vinegar comes to the boil, reduce the heat so you have a light bubble and carefully put the eggs into it. After about 3 minutes, remove eggs with a slotted spoon and rest the spoon and egg on kitchen paper to ensure no soggy eggs. When the asparagus is cooked, divide onto two serving plates, place two eggs on top of each, spoon over the Greek yoghurt and add the butter on to the asparagus tips, add a nice peice of warm crusty bread to your meal and enjoy.

JENNY'S ROAST LAMB FILLET

Mum's best roast, using local Isle of Wight lamb and seasonal root vegetables. Garlic and rosemary permeate the meat giving it a wonderful rich flavour. A great family Sunday lunch which can be served with our smoked garlic dauphinoise or classic roast potatoes. All the preparation of this dish can be done 24 hours in advance.

Serves 6

> "garlic and rosemary flavours permeate the meat"

Large fillet of Isle of Wight lamb
Selection of root vegetables, peeled and cubed, whatever is available, one of each: parsnips, sweet potatoes, swede, celeriac, turnip, carrots, butternut squash
3 tablespoons of extra-virgin olive oil
4 large sprigs of rosemary
1 bulb of garlic, cloves unpeeled
Sea salt

200ml stock (lamb, chicken, beef - whatever is available)
½ glass of red wine
1 tablespoon of redcurrant jelly
2 tablespoon of Greek yoghurt or crème fraîche

Prepare all the vegetables, toss in olive oil, a good sprinkling of sea salt and the rosemary sprigs in a large shallow roasting tin. If you like, you can then cover these and keep in the fridge if preparing for the next day. Pre-heat the oven to 220°C. Scatter half the garlic cloves amongst the vegetables. Peel and chop the remaining cloves into smaller slivers which can then be pushed into the lamb meat by first stabbing holes with a sharp knife. Rub the lamb with rosemary, olive oil and sea salt and squeeze in with the vegetables. After putting the dish in the oven, turn down to 200°C and roast for 30 minutes. To make a delicious sauce to enhance this dish, remove the lamb, cover with foil then tea towels and leave to rest. Scoop the vegetables into a serving bowl and keep warm.

Add the stock and the red wine to the juices remaining in the roasting pan, place on medium heat, scraping any bits from the bottom. Reduce until the alcohol has evaporated then stir in the redcurrant jelly and yoghurt or crème fraîche. The joint can then be carved and served with the vegetables and your choice of potatoes with the sauce drizzled over the meat.

ROASTED PURPLE-SPROUTING BROCCOLI

"serve as a side dish with a roast"

One of the best spring vegetables around and the garlic complements it perfectly.
You can serve as a side dish with a roast or any meat dish.

400g of purple-sprouting broccoli
2 tablespoons of vegetable oil or groundnut oil
2 tablespoons of toasted sesame oil
5 garlic cloves, crushed
1 tablespoon of toasted sesame seeds

Pre-heat oven to 180°C. Trim off any of the really hard bits of stem from the broccoli and lay it in a baking tray. Mix the oil, crushed garlic and sesame seeds, then pour over the brocolli and toss them all together. Place in the oven for 20-30 minutes until the broccoli has started to brown.

ROASTED ELEPHANT GARLIC SOUP

Elephant garlic is probably more closely related to the leek than to ordinary garlic. The bulbs are impressively large although in terms of flavour, elephant garlic is much less intense and sweeter. It has been described - rather unkindly - as "garlic for people who don't like garlic". It's true it hasn't got the kick of real garlic, but it does have a lovely flavour and works especially well roasted, as in this recipe. The basil purée sets off the flavour of the soup beautifully.

"the garlic for people who don't like garlic"

Serves 6

    2 bulbs of elephant garlic
    100ml of olive oil
    4 leeks, coarsely chopped
    1 onion, coarsely chopped
    1 or 2 large potatoes, peeled and coarsely chopped
    1 glass white wine
    1 litre of chicken or vegetable stock
    Salt and freshly ground black pepper

    For the basil purée:
    Handful of basil leaves
    100ml olive oil

Pre-heat oven to 220°C. Slice the top off the garlic bulbs just far enough down to cut into the flesh. Drizzle the top with olive oil, making sure it runs down into the cloves, then wrap them in foil and bake for about 1 hour or until soft and golden. Squeeze out the flesh from each individual garlic clove into a large saucepan then add a dash of olive oil, the leeks, onion, potato, and wine. Bring to the boil, reduce to a simmer, and cook until the wine has reduced to half its volume.

Add the stock, and salt and pepper, and simmer for 30 minutes, stirring occasionally. While the soup is cooking, make the basil purée. Blanch the basil leaves by placing them in boiling salted water for 15 to 20 seconds and then immediately plunging them into an ice-water bath. Remove and pat dry. Place basil leaves in the bowl of a food processor. Add salt. With the machine running, slowly drizzle in the oil until a smooth purée is formed, set aside. When the soup is cooked, cool slightly then purée the mixture in a blender until smooth. If the soup is too thick, thin by adding stock or water. Taste and adjust seasonings. Before serving drizzle a swirl of basil purée into the tops of the bowls.

GARLIC FARM CAFE TOASTED CIABATTA

"Purple Moldovan garlic creates real persistence of flavour"

By using Purple Moldovan garlic for this garlic bread you'll notice a real persistence of flavour with an amazing aroma.

2 Ciabatta slippers (normally about 8-10" in length)
3 fat cloves Purple Moldovan garlic
1 sprig fresh rosemary
125g Isle of Wight butter

Peel and finely chop the garlic, along with the rosemary. Soften the butter slightly and mix with the garlic and rosemary. Slice the bread lengthways and spread with the garlic butter. Place on a grill tray and grill till golden brown, cut and serve. Spice it up by adding a few red chilli flakes to the butter.

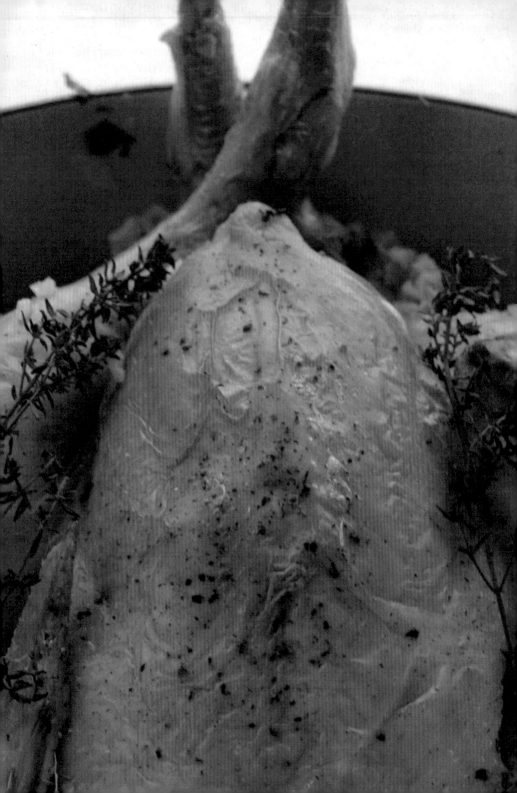

HAPPY CHICKEN
WITH LOADS OF CLOVES

"an entire meal in one pot"

The classic chicken with 40 cloves never fails to please. This is a slight variation which makes an entire meal in one pot. Of course, you can use as many cloves as you want so don't hold back. Do make sure you get a good quality free range chicken. Brownriggs Poultry produce wonderful birds and are usually at the Isle of Wight farmers' markets in Newport on a Friday morning or Ryde on a Saturday morning. No excuses not to buy a happy hen.

Serves 4

> 1 large free range chicken
> 500g brown rice
> 1 glass white wine
> Chopped parsley, bay leaves, thyme
> 2 carrots, chopped
> 2 slices bacon, chopped
> 2 onions, chopped
> Zest and juice of 2 lemons
> Peeled cloves from 3-4 bulbs of garlic
> or more if you like

Pre-heat oven to 180°C. Pour rice into a large casserole and stir in parsley, onions, carrots, bacon and lemon zest. Place the chicken on top and tip over the garlic, thyme and bay leaves. Squeeze the lemons on top and pop the skins in the cavity. Pour the wine into the rice and add water to cover it by about 2cm. Cover with the lid and place low in the oven for 1 ½ hours then remove the lid for the last half hour to brown the chicken and garlic. This is a brilliant one pot rustic dinner party dish, full of flavour and nutrition.

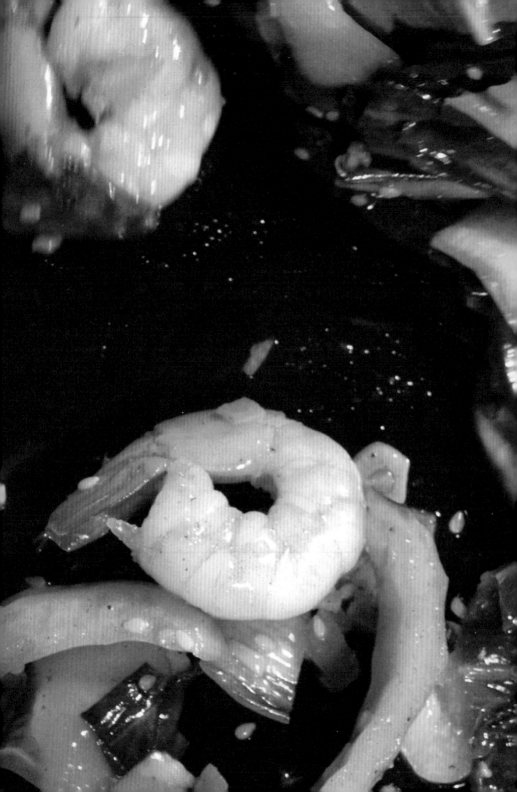

PRAWN AND
PAK CHOI STIR FRY

"**prawns take on garlic flavours very well**"

The crunchy nutty flavour of the pak choi works well with lots of sliced garlic. Prawns take on garlic flavours very well. This is a brilliant, very quick, mid-week supper with plenty of flavour.

Serves 4

300g large prawns, preferably tails on
2 pak choi, chopped into slices
4 cloves of garlic, sliced
Knob of ginger, grated or finely chopped
1 tablespoon of toasted sesame oil
2 tablespoons of rice bran oil (or other cooking oil)
2 teaspoons of Chinese five spice
1 teaspoon of Szechuan peppercorns
1 fresh red chilli (optional)

Heat the cooking oil in the wok then throw in the garlic, ginger, spices and peppercorns and cook for about one minute before quickly adding all the other ingredients, constantly tossing them in the wok. Cook until the prawns have turned pink and serve immediately with plain rice or noodles.

RABBIT, PANCETTA AND WILD GARLIC RISOTTO

"it is essential to marinate the rabbit meat before cooking"

Catching rabbits with Dad was one of our favourite evening activities as we were growing up. None of us could escape a lesson in gutting, pissing and potting. Even if catching rabbits isn't your thing, we'd be surprised if this brilliant combination of flavours doesn't get you hopping. It is essential to marinate the rabbit meat for at least 12 hours before cooking to tenderize it, preferably in buttermilk but you could use vinegar or salted water. If you haven't got access to any wild garlic then you can use extra normal garlic, green garlic or spring onions thrown in after cooking.

Serves 4

2 whole rabbits, skinned
6 shallots
1 carrot, roughly chopped
1 celery stick, roughly chopped
200g Arborio risotto rice
1 glass dry white wine
50g butter
3 cloves garlic, crushed
Handful of fresh flat-leaf parsley, chopped
100g pancetta, chopped into very small squares
Handful of wild garlic leaves, shredded
75g parmesan or any strong hard cheese

Rinse your marinated rabbit and place in a large pan of water along with the carrot, 2 shallots and the celery. Cover and simmer for up to 4 hours either on the hob or in the oven at about 120°C. Remove the rabbits from the stock and remove as much meat as possible from the bone, setting to one side. At the same time, fry the shallots, garlic and pancetta with butter until the shallots have softened. Add the rice and toast for a couple of minutes, stirring constantly. Pour in the wine and stir. Once the alcohol has evaporated, start to add the stock one ladle at a time stirring constantly. Keep adding stock until the rice is cooked and the risotto has creamy consistency. Now you can add the cheese, rabbit, parsley and wild garlic leaves. Stir well then serve with parmesan shavings and a few extra wild garlic leaves on top.

SUMMER

Recipes for summer

As the old Islanders say: "A day off the Isle of Wight is a day wasted." When the sun's shining down on the Arreton Valley, butterflies hover over the headlands, boats glide across the bay and there's a freshly harvested crop of garlic in the yard, we couldn't agree more.

The Island really comes into its own during this season creating a natural gravitational pull for a variety of people from music lovers, watersports fanatics, sailing enthusiasts and walkers to those who just want to kick back in a deckchair and breathe in that famous healing air on the south coast. At the Garlic Farm, summer is our most exciting and active season. The harvest, drying, cleaning and plaiting all take place during these long summer days. As well as an abundance of garlic to hand, there is also plenty of fresh local produce: Isle of Wight tomatoes and salads, corn on the cob, fresh fish and crab. And all ready to be washed down with our favourite brew: Ale of Wight from Goddards brewery. With long sunny days, barbecues and picnics in mind, here are our favourite sunshine recipes that give us the flavour of summer on the Island.

- Aubergine, courgette and halloumi stack
- Summer barbecue burgers
- Tortilla
- Marrow gratin
- Bubble and squeak with garlic scapes
- Broad bean and pea hummous
- Crispy couscous and herb chicken fillets
- The best cheesy garlic bread
- Baked rhubarb mackerel
- The Garlic Farm bruschetta
- Lamb kofte tortilla wraps

AUBERGINE, COURGETTE AND HALLOUMI STACK

Courgettes and aubergines are the flavour of summer and they soak up garlic flavours brilliantly. This makes a wonderful vegetarian dish or accompaniment to barbecued meats.

Serves 4

1 large aubergine, thinly sliced lengthways
2 courgettes, sliced lengthways
200g of halloumi cheese
5 garlic cloves
Good handful of fresh herbs, chopped (parsley, mint, thyme, oregano)
Extra virgin olive oil
Salt and pepper

Pre-heat the oven to 180°C. In a roasting tray, start by laying a couple of aubergine strips to make the base of the stack. Drizzle olive oil, crush over one clove of garlic, spread, then sprinkle over herbs, salt and pepper. (Don't add too much salt as the halloumi is quite salty.) Make the next layer from a few courgette strips, again drizzling over olive oil, herbs, salt and pepper. The next layer is halloumi in thin strips. Continue to stack until you have used all the vegetables- finish with a layer of halloumi drizzled with olive oil and sprinkled with herbs. Cover with foil and place in the oven for 20 minutes. Remove the foil and replace in the oven until the cheese has turned golden brown.

"courgettes soak up garlic flavours brilliantly"

SUMMER BARBECUE BURGERS

"bursting with flavour from Garlic Farm chutneys"

If you go to the trouble of lighting a barbecue it's worth having some excellent homemade burgers to put on it. These are very simple to make and bursting with flavour. You can use your choice of chutney in the mixture - these are just our suggestions.

500g lean steak mince
½ jar The Garlic Farm Apricot, garlic and ginger chutney or Garlic, tomato and ginger chutney
1 red onion finely chopped
4 cloves garlic
1 large egg or 2 small ones
A good bunch of mixed fresh herbs (parsley, coriander, chives and thyme all work)
Salt and pepper to taste

Mix the ingredients together well. Roll into balls and flatten with your hand to size to fit your buns, remembering there will always be a little shrinkage. Barbecue and don't burn unless you like that frazzled flavour.

TORTILLA

Great hot when it's just made, sliced into a sandwich or cold with a salad, fantastic to have just ready in the fridge for a little nibble.

Serves 4 - 6 as a main dish

> 2 onions, sliced
> 6 eggs
> 3 cloves of garlic
> 1 teaspoon of sweet paprika
> A squirt of tomato purée
> 500g of potatoes
> Half a bag of spinach

Pre-heat oven to 180°C. In a large frying pan, soften the onions slowly in olive oil with a little water and a lid over them to allow them to cook well before browning. Towards the end add the garlic so that it doesn't lose too much of its kick. Thinly slice the potatoes and bake in the oven with some more olive oil and salt for about 30 minutes. Beat together the eggs and purée. When the onions are ready, throw in paprika and chopped spinach, stir together with potatoes and eggs. Allow to settle into shape and cook on the top on a low heat for about 10 minutes then, depending on your pan, you can put it under the grill or into the oven to finish off.

"have it ready in the fridge for a little nibble"

MARROW GRATIN

Delicious marrow, quite hard to come by and with an unworthy reputation of not being very tasty but actually a lovely flavour and texture.

Serves 4

1 marrow
8 generous slices of Isle of Wight ham
200g of grated gruyère cheese
A handful of breadcrumbs
2-3 cloves of garlic
A knob of butter
200ml milk
2 tablespoons of flour (rice flour works very well)

Pre-heat oven to 180°C. Halve the marrow and scoop out the seeds. Peel, slice and lightly steam for about 5 minutes. Fry the garlic in butter, add flour and cook for a minute or two, then slowly add the milk, stirring continuously to avoid lumping, then finish with some of the marrow steaming water and allow to thicken. Stir in the cheese to the sauce then pour over the marrow, sprinkle with crumbs and bake until golden. Serve with slices of ham.

"lovely flavour and texture"

BUBBLE AND SQUEAK WITH GARLIC SCAPES

"scapes are not dissimilar to chives"

Scapes are the stems and flower buds sometimes also called rocamboles, that emerge from hard neck garlic varieties and elephant garlic. (See our section on growing garlic for more information). Scapes are not dissimilar to chives and can be used in salad or stir fries. Their delicate but distinctive flavour complements this traditional vegetable dish. Save a few scapes for decorating the dish - they look beautiful and very unusual.

> Cooked mashed potato
> Cooked carrots, cabbage, sprouts, and
> typically any other green vegetable available
> 1 bunch garlic scapes (about 6)
> Olive oil and butter for frying

Gently fry the vegetables in the oil and butter in a large heavy frying pan. Add the scapes cut up into 2 cm lengths and stir fry for a couple of minutes. Gradually incorporate the mashed potato and season generously. Press down all the ingredients until gold and crispy and then toss over and brown the other side. Serve with garlic sausages and a garlicky tomato sauce.

BROAD BEAN AND PEA HUMMOUS

This is a much fresher alternative to the classic chickpea hummous. The fresher your ingredients, the better the flavours for this zesty little appetiser but if you can't get fresh broad beans you can use frozen (but definitely not tinned!) Serve with our garlic bites or any crisps for dipping.

"fresher alternative to classic hummous"

300g broad beans, shelled and boiled
(no need to remove bean skins)
100g peas (best fresh but can use frozen)
4-5 large garlic cloves, crushed
100g of crème fraîche
2 tablespoons of extra virgin olive oil
Handful of mint
Juice of one lemon
Salt and freshly ground black pepper

Throw all the ingredients except the crème fraîche in a blender and blend until smooth. Add the crème fraîche, stirring not too rapidly or it will go runny. Garnish with a couple of mint leaves.

CRISPY COUS COUS & HERB CHICKEN FILLETS

Serves 4 as a starter

2 large skinless chicken fillets
2 eggs
150ml of milk
Small cup of plain flour
2 cups of dry uncooked cous cous
1 cup natural colour breadcrumbs
1 dessert spoon dry mixed herbs
1 dessert spoon cumin seeds
Salt and pepper

For the mayonnaise
2 egg yolks
1 teaspoon English mustard
500ml sunflower oil
180ml extra virgin olive oil
3 dessert spoons of white wine vinegar
1 bunch fresh chives
6 Solent Wight garlic cloves

"great
dipped
into garlic
mayonnaise"

Cut each chicken fillet into 4 nice sized strips. Prepare for coating the chicken by pouring some flour on a plate, beating the eggs and milk together in a bowl and mixing the couscous, breadcrumbs, cumin seeds, salt, pepper and herbs in another bowl. Lightly roll the chicken strips first in the flour and shake off excess then dip in the egg and finally throw in cous cous bowl to coat well but still shake off excess. Place on a plate and keep in the fridge until ready.

Make your garlic mayo: in a food blender put together garlic, chives and mustard, whizz until chopped and reasonably smooth, on a steady speed. Slowly pour in the olive and sunflower oils, be careful not to add too quickly otherwise it might split. Once all the oil is mixed in, add the vinegar and salt and pepper to taste, and you should end up with a nice thick chive green mayo ready for your crispy chicken fillets. Refrigerate until needed. Back to the chicken, if you have a deep fat fryer with good clean oil turn it on up to about 175°C, put the chicken in and cook until golden and floating near the top, this is a good indicator as to whether it will be cooked or not. If you don't have a fat fryer then bake in the oven, which is a slightly healthier option. Serve with a mixed crunchy leaf salad with a squeeze of lemon juice and the chive green garlic mayonnaise for dipping.

THE BEST
CHEESY GARLIC BREAD

It's the staple garlic side order. We take our garlic bread pretty seriously. We've tried and tested so many variations and only the best make the grade. This one takes garlic bread to a whole new level. You don't have to add the cheese if you prefer the purist version. The paprika adds the perfect final touch for flavour and colour. You won't get a better one.

1 baguette
100g butter
3-4 large garlic cloves crushed
100g mozzarella ball
100g any hard strong cheese (cheddar works well)
Handful of any combination of fresh parsley, rosemary, basil or marjoram
Paprika for sprinkling

Pre-heat the oven to 200°C. Take all the filling ingredients, place them into a food processor and blend until completely mixed. Cut the bread into diagonal slices about 2/3 of the way through so the loaf stays intact. Use a flat knife to spread the filling generously in between the slices.Place the loaf on to a large piece of kitchen foil and wrap loosely sealing the ends and top. (You may need to break the loaf in half to fit in the oven). Bake for about 20-25 minutes, until all the filling is melted. For the last five minutes you can open the foil, sprinkle on the paprika and brown the top.
Serve immediately.

"the staple garlic side order"

BAKED
RHUBARB MACKEREL

Certain foods complement each other, like colours,
they enhance each others' qualities: spinach and
orange, apple and cinnamon, rhubarb and mackerel.
Find the freshest mackerel you can lay your hands on,
preferably just fished by you from the sea. Working
for your supper always makes it taste immeasurably
better. On this theme, if you can pluck rhubarb from
your own garden you will of course add to the overall
pride and satisfaction felt in presenting this otherwise
very easy dish.

To serve two as a starter

> "find the
> freshest
> mackerel
> you can
> lay your
> hands on"

- 1 mackerel, filleted by you or your fishmonger
- 1 sweet potato, cut into 8 wedges
- 1 stick of rhubarb, cut into 8 lengths
- 4 teaspoons of Rhubarb and Pear Chutney
- 3 teaspoons of chopped rosemary
- 2 cloves of garlic
- 2 handfuls of rocket tossed in lemon juice and olive oil

Pre-heat the oven to 200ºC. Toss the sweet potato
wedges and rhubarb in olive oil and place on a baking
tray lined with baking parchment, this way they don't
stick, get a lovely colour and it saves on washing up.
It's possible to buy reusable baking parchment which is
obviously kinder on the environment as well as being
brilliant at doing the job. Pop in the oven near but not
at the top, for about 20 to 30 minutes until they have
slightly browned and basically cooked. Test by giving
them a poke to see if they're soft. Meanwhile, heap 2
teaspoons of chutney on each of the fillets, sprinkle
with rosemary and squeeze on the garlic through a
crusher, making sure to scrape out the crusher as well.
Place on the tray with the potato and rhubarb and pop
back in the oven for 10 minutes at the most. Serve on
the bed of rocket with an extra squeeze of lemon over
the top.

THE GARLIC FARM BRUSCHETTA

"keep your guests happy while you light the barbecue"

The Italians really know what they're talking about when it comes to using garlic. A glass of cold Sauvignon Blanc and a few bruschetta will definitely keep your guests happy while you light the barbecue. You can vary the toppings but these classics are a good place to start.

1 loaf ciabatta or baguette
3-4 large garlic cloves, peeled
400g of very ripe flavoursome plum tomatoes
1 red onion
Handful of basil leaves
1 jar of black pitted olives (crespo are good)
1 red chilli
Some white anchovies that melt in your mouth
Plenty of extra virgin olive oil

Slice the bread slightly on the diagonal to make larger slices. Drizzle or, with a pastry brush lightly coat the bread on both sides with olive oil. Pop them in the oven until golden, about 10 minutes. Remove and, while still hot, rub with a peeled clove of garlic on one side, then add your topping.

For the tomato topping, first peel them by scoring a cross on the top of the tomato and putting in boiling water for 5-10 mins. The skin should just slip off but you don't want soggy tomatoes. Cut into dice and remove the seeds, mix with diced onion and pour over some olive oil. Shred some basil, toss together, spoon the mixture over the bread and eat.

For the olive tapenade just blend the olives with olive oil and spread on.

All bruschetta need a good twist of black pepper.

For a cheating easy topping, try using Garlic Farm pesto.

LAMB KOFTE TORTILLA WRAPS

Fantastic for a picnic, take a pot of delicious tomatoey balls, crème fraîche, grated cheese, coriander and some lettuce. Great fun to assemble on a rug, either in tortilla or a leaf of iceberg or little gem lettuce.

To make 4 generous wraps

For the kofte:
500g of lamb mince
3 large crushed garlic cloves
1 fresh red chilli chopped
A handful each of chopped coriander and mint
Zest and juice of 1 lemon
1 teaspoon each of toasted cumin
and coriander seeds
1 teaspoon of smoked paprika
Salt

For the sauce:
½ large onion
½ tablespoon of tomato purée
1 can of chopped tomatoes

To make the wraps:
4 or more ready-made wholemeal tortilla wraps
Iceberg lettuce, shredded
More coriander to taste
Grated cheddar cheese
Crème fraîche

"great fun to assemble on a picnic rug"

Put all ingredients together for the kofte, roll into balls in your hands and fry in a dry pan as there is plenty of fat coming out of the lamb. Remove from the pan and, keeping the fat, fry the onions until softened then add the purée and the chopped tomatoes. Cook for about 10 minutes so it keeps a light fresh taste. Place a few kofte in a wrap, cover with a good spoonful of sauce then sprinkle with cheese, coriander and a handful of shredded lettuce. Top with crème fraîche.
Wrap and enjoy.

THE SEASONS
AUTUMN

Recipes for autumn

It's the witching season! Of course, we don't tend to worry about that at the Garlic Farm. No vampire would dare come near us. It's a good idea to stock up on your garlic in the autumn and also start planting some early varieties.

Apart from carving out our pumpkins, this time of year sees our team in the production kitchen working at full capacity to increase the stocks of pickles, chutneys and relishes. Arguably it's the best time of year for vegetables with plenty of luscious roots around to which garlic makes the best accompaniment whether combined in a soup or roasted until you can squeeze out the juicy flesh.

Columbine, who has been the creative chef behind many of the recipes in this book, has a little cooking mantra: "colour equals flavour" and that couldn't be more appropriate for our autumnal selection of garlic recipes. Soak up beautifully rich autumn colours and flavours with all these wonderfully tasty garlic-ful dishes.

- Spanish chicken hotpot
- Pumpkin and garlic halloween soup
- Beef bourgignon
- Spicy Moroccan lamb cous cous
- Thai fish pie
- The Garlic Farm carbonara
- Whole roasted cloves with roasted roots
- Oak-smoked garlic mushroom and bacon stack
- Garlic bites

SPANISH CHICKEN HOTPOT

This is a rich garlic and fennel based dish given an extra depth and boost of flavour by the nutty and delicious Oloroso sherry. In cooking it becomes rich and spicy. The garlic needs to be abundant to compete with feisty fennel and both are then tamed by the soothing tomato and sprinkling of parsley to freshen at the end. Great soaked into anything from mash, baked potato, rice or couscous.

Serves 4

> "garlic needs to be abundant to compete with feisty fennel"

10 cloves garlic, peeled and squashed a bit
One whole bulb of fennel finely sliced
or chopped on a mandolin
4 thighs and 4 legs of chicken with bones and skin
2 cartons of chopped tomatoes
1 tablespoon tomato purée
1 tablespoon of fennel seeds
1 teaspoon of sweet smoked paprika
1 large glass of medium Oloroso sherry
(all for the pot - have a separate glass
for yourself with a cube of ice)
½ tablespoon vegetable bouillon (Marigold is good)
Rice bran oil or sunflower oil

Pre-heat the oven to 200°C.

Brown the chicken skin side down in your pot with half the fennel seeds using a tablespoon of rice bran oil. Toss the fennel with some oil and the rest of the seeds and roast in the pre-heated oven for half an hour checking and turning half way. When the chicken has browned, add the garlic to gain its own colour, add the paprika and then the Oloroso. Let this bubble until the alcohol has burned off, you will know because when you smell it, it will hurt your nose if it's too early. Then in with the tomato, bouillon and fennel, give a little stir and cover. Let it simmer for at least an hour until the chicken is falling off the bone. If it still has a lot of liquid after an hour, take the lid off and let it reduce. Sprinkle the parsley and eat.

PUMPKIN AND GARLIC HALLOWEEN SOUP

"hot and spicy ghoul deterrent"

A good hot and spicy soup for Halloween. Can be adapted for other seasons by using any other available squash such as butternut or just by using sweet potato.

Serves 4

Flesh from one medium-sized pumpkin
One large sweet potato, peeled and chopped
One large onion
4-6 cloves garlic
One small chilli
Small piece of ginger (grated)
One pint of chicken or vegetable stock
2 tablespoons of crème fraîche
Handful of chopped parsley or sage to serve
Olive oil
Salt and pepper

Chop the onion and soften in one tablespoon of olive oil. Add the sweet potato and then the stock. Cook for 15 minutes until soft then add the pumpkin flesh, chopped chilli, grated ginger and peeled garlic cloves. Cover and simmer till cooked. Add the herbs and season to taste. Blend then add crème fraîche to serve.

BEEF BOURGIGNON

Mum has adapted this much loved family favourite from the traditional French recipe. It is extremely versatile and is always better made the day before which allows the flavours to intensify. Use a heavy based casserole that can be used on the hob and inside the oven.

"works well with our dauphinoise"

Serves 6

200g of unsmoked streaky bacon cut into small pieces
1.5kg of lean stewing steak (cubed)
1 tablespoon of olive oil
1 carrot, diced
1 onion, diced
1 tablespoon of flour
½ bottle of red wine
¾ pint of beef stock
Garlic – a whole bulb – several cloves
peeled and crushed, and a few left whole
Bouquet garni/herbes de provence/bay leaf
2 dozen button mushrooms
1 dozen baby shallots
Salt and pepper

Pre-heat oven to 150°C.

Sauté the bacon, onion, and carrot in the olive oil until soft, then remove from the pan and add the cubed meat. Brown the meat then stir in the flour, salt and pepper. Add red wine and stock and bring to the boil. Add the onion, carrot, herbs and garlic. Cover and cook in a slow oven for at least 3 hours. Sauté the mushrooms, whole garlic cloves and shallots in butter until shallots soften, then add to the casserole and cook for a further 30 minutes. If the sauce is too thin, strain the meat and bring the liquid to the boil and reduce. Serve with your choice of potatoes. Works well with our dauphinoise for a really rich supper.

SPICY MOROCCAN LAMB COUS COUS

"one of Jo's treats for hungry surfers"

My sister Jo grew up in the Garlic Farm kitchen, watching over Jenny's shoulder as she toiled away at the Aga, meal after delicious meal for her ever expanding family. Now running a restaurant out in Morocco, feeding hungry surfer boys on the beach front of a small surf town, Jo has taken her knowledge of traditional English country grub and combined it with the Moroccan traditions of hearty tagines, cous cous feasts and meaty grills resulting in delicious, wholesome food, guaranteed to please and always plentiful.

Serves 4-6

Extra virgin olive oil
1 kilo of diced lamb
100g of seasoned flour
1 large aubergine, chopped chunkily
1 courgette, chopped in large chunks
2 carrots, peeled and chopped in thick batons
1 large red onion
1 red pepper, cut into 2cm squares
1 whole garlic bulb, peeled and crushed
1 large red chilli, finely chopped
1 large bunch of fresh coriander, chopped
1 tablespoon of ground cumin
1 tablespoon of paprika
1 teaspoon of cinnamon
1 tin of chopped tomatoes
3 tablespoons of tomato purée
1 pint of lamb stock
(or any other good stock available)

500g of medium cous cous
Vegetable stock - enough to cover the cous cous
Handful of fresh coriander, parsley and mint, chopped
Salt and black pepper

Toss the lamb in flour to coat it. Heat the oil and then braise the lamb until all is brown in colour. Set aside.

Sauté onions in oil with paprika, cumin and cinnamon, add the garlic and chilli with a little more oil or water if necessary so as not to burn the garlic. When softened, return the meat to the pan and add the tomatoes, tomato purée, stock, salt and pepper to taste. Bring to the boil and then let everything simmer for 1 hour. If the meat is on the bone or tough, it may need a little longer.

Put the chopped aubergine, carrots, courgette and pepper on a roasting tray and toss with olive oil and a sprinkling more of the spices. Roast, turning every now and then for about 45 minutes at 170°C until browned and sweet.

Whilst the stew is simmering, make the herby cous cous. Place cous cous in a dry saucepan and toast on the hob stirring quite regularly until it has reached various tones of brown, this gives it a much fuller nutty flavour. Pour over the boiling vegetable stock so that it covers all the cous cous, cover for 5 minutes until the water is all soaked up, then run through the cous cous with a fork to fluff it up. Add all the chopped coriander, parsley and mint.

Serve the lamb stew on top of the herby cous cous. If the stew is very spicy, serve with a bowl of natural yoghurt on the side.

"serve with natural yoghurt on the side"

THAI FISH PIE

"easy and flavoursome - non-dairy too"

I made this for a non-dairy friend and then discovered it was delicious in its own right. Full of flavour and fairly economical.

Serves 4-6

1 can of coconut milk
4 lime leaves (fresh if possible, they keep very well in the freezer but are not so good dried)
1 large fillet of haddock, skinned, boned and cut into good size chunks
6 strips of unsmoked streaky bacon
1 large onion, diced
4 cloves of garlic, chopped
1 thumb of chopped ginger
1 carrot, diced
1 parsnip, diced
½ a bag of raw spinach
1 tablespoon of rice bran oil
4 potatoes, peeled and halved
2 sweet potatoes, peeled and quartered

Pre-heat the oven to 180°C. Bring the coconut milk to just before the boil with the lime leaves and set to one side to infuse. Put the bacon, onion, garlic, ginger, carrot and parsnip, tossed with a little rice bran oil on a baking tray and roast until browned, about 30 minutes. Into a ceramic dish put the raw fish and spinach, toss with the other vegetables, stir in the infused coconut milk, including the leaves, just remember not to eat them. Boil and strain the potatoes and mash together; the sweet potatoes are gluey enough to bind it but of course add some butter if you like.
Spoon the potato over the fish mixture and pop in the oven for 20-30 minutes.

THE GARLIC FARM CARBONARA

This classic dish is made particularly delicious by a large helping of garlic. You can get Isle of Wight free range eggs with rich yellow yolks from any of the farm shops on the Island.

Serves 4

500g of good spaghetti or other pasta
(if you can get fresh it's always best)
4 fat cloves of garlic, finely chopped
2 shallots, finely chopped
6 thick slices of pancetta or streaky bacon, chopped into small pieces
4 large free range eggs
100 ml of double cream
40g of freshly grated parmesan
Olive oil
2 spring onions, chopped
Handful of basil, chopped
Handful of parsley, chopped
Freshly ground black pepper

Bring a large pan of water to the boil and if using dried, add the pasta, cooking according to instructions. If using fresh pasta, wait until the sauce is prepared before cooking. You need to make sure the eggs are added while the pasta is hot. In a large frying pan, fry the bacon or pancetta, shallots and garlic in a dollop of olive oil for about 5-7 minutes. Put eggs, cream and most of the cheese into a bowl and beat with a good amount of black pepper. When the pasta is cooked, drain then return to the pan off the heat. Quickly add the shallots, bacon and garlic and the egg mixture, stirring well. Add the spring onions, basil and parsley and stir well again. Serve immediately with extra parmesan and freshly ground black pepper on top.

"a classic made extra delicious by a large helping of garlic"

WHOLE ROASTED CLOVES WITH ROASTED ROOTS

The perfect accompaniment to your roast lamb. The longer and slower this is cooked, the sweeter and more flavoursome the vegetables become. The garlic cloves will be completely softened and squeezing out the flesh is immensely satisfying, not to mention the taste.

Serves 4

> 3 large carrots, cut into thick strips
> 3 large parsnips, cut into thick strips
> 1 swede, cut into small chunks
> 6-8 large garlic cloves, unpeeled
> Sprig or two of thyme
> 3 tablespoons of rice bran oil or sunflower oil

Pre-heat the oven to 200°C if cooking fast and 170°C if cooking slow. Throw all the ingredients into a roasting tin or dish and toss well in the oil. Roast in oven for 30 minutes at the higher temperature or 1 hour 30 minutes at the lower temperature.

"squeezing out the roasted garlic flesh is immensely satisfying"

OAK-SMOKED GARLIC MUSHROOM AND BACON STACK

Who can resist the mouth watering aroma of garlic and bacon sizzling in a pan on a brisk autumn morning? Big fat Portobello mushrooms are the best for this if you can't get to any field mushrooms but in the end any will do. If they are earthy never wash them in water as this makes them slimy, instead wipe them with a bit of dry kitchen paper. A little earth adds to the flavour.

"a little earth on your mushrooms adds to the flavour"

Serves 2

> 2 field or Portobello mushrooms
> Half a tub of oak smoked garlic butter (sounds a lot but it's too good to scrimp on)
> A handful of rough chopped parsley
> Back bacon
> 2 large free range eggs
> Vampire Relish, Garlic, Tomato and Ginger Chutney or any of the Garlic Farm mustards -
> It all depends on how you're feeling, fiery, fruity or fairly traditional
> Slices of thick crusty bread
> Parsley to garnish

Grill the bacon to reduce the fat rather than frying as there's plenty going on with the butter. Grill as much as you like. I like it crispy but still meaty rather than cindered but some like it rarer. Melt the butter, slice the mushrooms long and thin or thick as desired and fry. Remove mushrooms when they're done, about 5 to 10 minutes and using the same butter, fry your egg. Assemble in the bread that you have spread with your chosen chutney or mustard, sprinkle parsley on top and munch, yum.

GARLIC BITES

"a great way to get garlic into the kids' diet"

These will vanish off the table as quick as a vampire disappears on a sunny day. The idea sprang from wanting to create a delicious and robust dipper for our garlic relishes and chutneys. They also make a great base for canapés. I've used wholemeal flour as a healthier option but you can use white flour if you prefer. If you've got little ones, these are a brilliant way to get garlic into their diet and their hands into cooking.

Makes 20 small biscuits

120g of self-raising flour, wholemeal or white
60g of butter, softened
60g of cheese, mature cheddar or similar
2-3 large cloves of garlic, crushed
½ teaspoon of dry mustard powder
1 tablespoon of cold water
Salt and pepper to taste

Pre-heat the oven to 220°C. Sift the flour into a large mixing bowl and add the mustard powder and crushed garlic. Mix together, then rub in the butter and grate in the cheese, a little at a time. Once all the butter and cheese is mixed in, season to taste, then add enough water to make the mixture stick together in a ball. Roll out the mixture on to a floured surface to about ½ cm thick then cut into either long fingers or squares as you prefer. Place on a greased baking tray and bake for 10-15 minutes at 220°C.

WINTER

Recipes for winter

The best thing about cold and crisp winter days is that they justify big, hearty meals. The sea is wild, the countryside is rugged and the fire is roaring in our shop and café.

The Island has lots of good game on offer and now is the time to try to get your hands on a pigeon or two for a rich pigeon pate or impress your dinner guests with our hugely popular wood pigeon Kievs.

You may not have considered it, but garlic is a brilliant way to jazz up your sprouts, works wonders in a gratin and is the perfect complement to all your winter meat dishes.

- Rich slow cooked bolognese
- Pigeon paté
- Ventnor rock salmon fish fingers
- Hearty lentil pie
- Gran's spicy beef pie
- Oak-smoked garlic dauphinoise
- Charlie's Garlic Farm meatloaf
- Butternut squash Sunday supper
- Garlic Farm wood pigeon kievs
- Braised shoulder of pork in prune juice

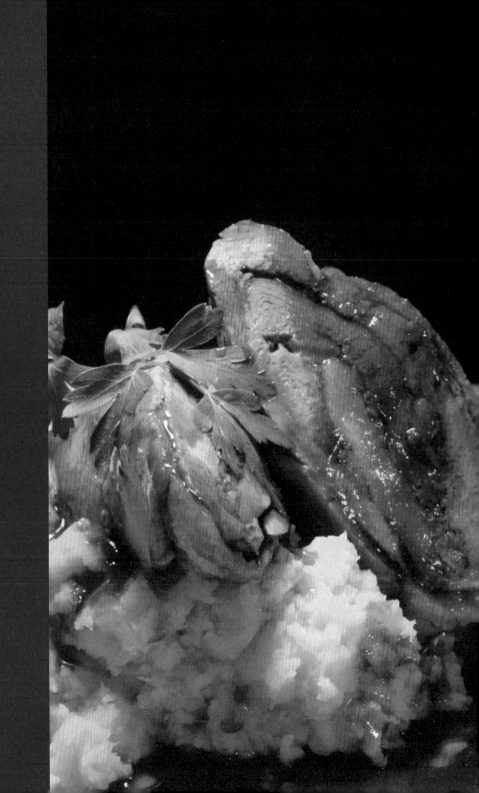

RICH SLOW COOKED BOLOGNESE

This takes time but not so much effort. It just needs you to be hanging around in the kitchen doing other things and occasionally giving it a stir but the result is so worth it and you can make as much as your pan will hold and freeze what is not consumed.

Serves 6-8

4 large onions, sliced or diced
3 carrots, diced
A bulb of garlic, cloves peeled
8 garlic cloves, crushed
A big bunch of fresh herbs with parsley, sage, rosemary, chives, fennel fronds, tarragon, anything green and herby, chopped
A teaspoon of fennel seeds
1 kg of minced beef, preferably lean
1 pack of tasty pork sausages, slit down the middle and the meat removed from their skins
2 tins of chopped tomatoes
1 large tablespoon of tomato purée
2 large glasses of red wine
1 large teaspoon of vegetable bouillon powder

"a great sauce for pasta, in a cottage pie or stuffed into a marrow"

Put the onions in a casserole with a knob of butter, a drizzle of olive oil and the fennel seeds and cover with the lid to let them slowly sweat, soften and caramelise. On low heat with occasional stirring this can take half an hour. The carrots and whole garlic cloves need roasting at 200°C in a tray for half an hour. When you remove the tray from the oven, keep it near the casserole because you can toss everything in there once it's prepared. Throw the softened onions in with the carrots. Brown the beef in the casserole in batches and make sure it's really brown with crispy bits rather than beige to get maximum flavour. Brown the sausage meat and really break it up, then add the crushed garlic and, 2 minutes later, the tomato purée. Give this 5 to 10 minutes to caramelise together, stirring fairly regularly and then add the wine and allow it to bubble and reduce.

Now add all the cooked ingredients back in, together with the tomatoes and bouillon. Put the lid on and simmer for about an hour then take the lid off and continue to simmer for about another hour until it is rich and delicious. This is great as a sauce for pasta, in a cottage pie, stuffed in a marrow - add a bit of chilli and some kidney beans and the possibilities become endless. The work is definitely worth it.

PIGEON PATE

"a good way to get rid of a glut of pigeons"

Made in a similar way to chicken liver paté. Don't be put off by the large quantity of fat. This is necessary because the pigeon breasts are very dense and lean. It is delicious with many of the Garlic Farm Chutneys – particularly Apricot, Garlic and Ginger or Fig and Apple. This recipe is a great way of making sense of a glut of pigeons without the laborious task of plucking and drawing the whole bird.

Makes one large paté

> 10 pigeon breasts, cubed
> 100g of lard
> 100g of butter
> 1 onion, peeled and chopped
> About 6 large cloves of garlic
> Fresh thyme/marjoram or winter savoury (chopped)
> 2 tablespoons of port
> 100g unsmoked bacon
> 6 crushed juniper berries
> Extra butter to cover
> Salt and pepper

Soften the butter and lard in a heavy-based saucepan. Add the chopped bacon and onion and sauté gently for about 5 minutes. Add the chopped pigeon breasts and sauté for about 10 minutes, being careful not to over-cook the meat; it should still be a little pink inside. Add the garlic, port, herbs, juniper berries and seasoning and, bringing quickly to the boil, transfer to a blender or food processor and blend until smooth. Pour into a dish or several small pots or ramekins. Melt the remaining butter and pour over the paté mixture. Chill before serving. Can be frozen.

VENTNOR ROCK
SALMON FISH FINGERS

"Ventnor fisheries sell a great variety of fresh fish"

Along the beach wall at Ventnor is a great fishmonger in a small blue hut selling a great variety of fresh fish, including lobster, crab, scallops and rock salmon. Rock salmon is a firm meaty fish, very good for a Thai green curry or for fishfingers. Up the coast it apparently has many names and comes under many guises but is, at the moment, in plentiful supply, unlike cod or haddock.

As much fish as you want, cut into fishfinger size strips (rock salmon can be replaced by monkfish if unobtainable)
Garlic Farm Garlic and Horseradish mustard
A piece of stale bread
2 tablespoons of toasted mixed seeds, sesame, pumpkin and sunflower
Zest of one lemon
A tablespoon of chopped parsley

In a blender or food processor crumb your bread, mince the seeds and add the zest and parsley. Generously cover the fingers in Garlic and Horseradish Mustard. Coat them well in the crumbs and place on baking sheet in the oven at 200°C for 20 minutes until slightly browned and crispy. Squeeze on lemon juice and possibly dip in Toasted Garlic Mayonnaise. Eat immediately, very moreish. Thinking of kids however, they make great finger food if you are slightly more sparing with the mustard. Cook them and take them cold as a picnic.

HEARTY LENTIL PIE

There's no need to even tell the steak lover that there's no meat in this dish as they won't miss it for a second. This can be simplified but equally anyone who finds it hard to fit in their five a day vegetables will be relieved to know they are all covered and more in this one pot recipe.

Serves 6

    4 sliced red onions
    Good knob of butter and a tablespoon of olive oil
    1 tablespoon of ground cumin
    1 tablespoon of ground coriander
    A large glass of red wine
    1 bulb of garlic, broken into peeled cloves
    2 carrots, cut into medium chunks
    2 tins of green lentils
    2 tablespoons of Garlic Farm
    Sweet Tomato, Garlic and Herb Chutney
    1 heaped teaspoon of vegetable bouillon
    1 bag of fresh spinach, chopped (must be fresh
    as the liquid given off is essential to the sauce)
    1 parsnip
    ½ a small swede
    3 medium potatoes
    4 heaped tablespoons of grated mature cheddar
    Milk and butter for mash

Pre-heat the oven to 200°C

"the meat lovers won't miss meat in this dish for a second"

Peel, chop a bit and boil all together the potatoes, parsnip and swede for the mash. Throw onions in a heavy bottomed casserole that can go in the oven, with butter and olive oil, put on the lid and soften slowly, adding a little water if they stick at all but they should have enough of their own moisture to sweat in. Put the garlic cloves and carrots in a baking tray and roast for half an hour.

Drain and mash the root vegetables with butter, milk, pepper and 3 tablespoons of the cheese, add salt to taste. When the onions have softened and slightly caramelised, pour in the wine and reduce until it loses the alcohol that goes up your nose. Add garlic, carrots, lentils, confit, bouillon, and spinach. Top with mash, sprinkle on the last tablespoon of cheese and either keep like this in the fridge to use later in the day or the next day, ready to go, or pop straight in the oven for 45 minutes, near the bottom until the top has slightly browned.

GRAN'S SPICY BEEF PIE

Paddy Bradshaw, our brilliant grandmother, used to cook in a good old-fashioned English style. We've done our best to recreate this classic of hers although we know that only our Gran could give it that special something. If you don't make it too spicy, the whole family will love this very easy and tasty pie.

Serves 6

One packet of ready-to-roll puff pastry
1 large onion, diced
1 large knob of butter
500g lean mince beef
150ml beef stock
3-4 cloves of Solent Wight garlic, crushed
1-3 teaspoons of medium curry powder, adjust to taste
1 tablespoon tomato purée
1 teaspoon Worcestershire sauce
Milk for glazing

Pre-heat oven to 220°C.

Soften and brown the onion in butter then add the crushed garlic for a minute before adding the mince. Brown all the mince to seal in the flavour before adding the stock, tomato purée, curry powder and Worcestershire sauce. Line a pie dish, or a series of individual pie dishes or ramekins with puff pastry and prick the base. Fill with the meat mixture and cover with remaining pastry and prick the top. Brush with milk and bake for 20 minutes. Serve hot with chips and fresh vegetables or cold with a salad.

"our brilliant grandmother Paddy cooked in a good-old fashioned English style"

OAK-SMOKED GARLIC DAUPHINOISE

Always a winner for a dinner party, this rich, classy dish is the best complement to juicy roasted lamb or beef. The smoky after-taste is wonderfully surprising. You can make it with normal unsmoked garlic if you don't have smoked garlic to hand. You won't need quite as much as with the milder smoked variety. The thinner the potato slices, the better - use a mandolin if you have one or just slice thinly with a sharp knife.

"rich and classy dinner party pleaser"

1kg of waxy firm potatoes, thinly sliced
500ml of full cream milk or mixed milk with cream
6 fat cloves oak-smoked garlic
1 teaspoon of nutmeg
50g of butter
Sea salt & freshly ground pepper

Pre-heat the over to 190°C.

Lay half the sliced potato in an oven-proof dish. Cover with a layer of seasoning then grate the garlic cloves on top. Tip the rest of the potato slices into the dish, spreading out evenly. Season again then pour over the milk and cream. Bake until all the liquid has been absorbed and the top has browned, usually about 1 - 1 ½ hours. Serve alongside a good portion of meat and green vegetables.

CHARLIE'S GARLIC FARM MEATLOAF

This hunky chunky meal is one of Charlie's real winners in the Garlic Farm Café. The colours and tastes are perfect for a blustery winter day. The black pudding gives a rich deep background for the sweet and flavoursome chutney. It's easy to make and freezes well so you can save it as a treat when returning from a cold and wet winter walk.

"one of Charlie's real winners"

Serves 4-6

> 250g chunky diced black pudding
> 2 500g sticks of good quality sausage meat
> 2 medium diced red onions
> 8 Solent Wight garlic cloves, minced
> 2 fresh sprigs of rosemary and sage, chopped
> 1 pot of Garlic Farm Garlic, Apricot & Ginger Chutney
> 4 slices of wholemeal breadcrumbs
> Maldon salt & ground black pepper

Dice the red onion and mince the garlic cloves and gently fry till golden brown in a little sunflower oil. In a bowl put the sausage meat, chopped black pudding, fresh breadcrumbs, a little seasoning, herbs and chutney. Add the red onions and garlic and mix well until it all comes together in one sticky mass, Put the sausage mixture in to the loaf tin and bake in a moderate oven for about 35 minutes. Test with a clean knife blade into the centre of the loaf; if it comes out clean, it's cooked. Turn out of the loaf tin on to a chopping board and cut into thick slices and serve as a main dish, maybe with buttered caramelised red onion and sweet potato mash and steamed savoy cabbage hearts, or just as a rustic lunch with some olive oil, black peppered rocket leaves and oak roasted IOW cherry tomatoes.

BUTTERNUT SQUASH SUNDAY SUPPER

"easy, healthy, flavoursome supper"

Very easy and a little healthy boost to start the week or finish the weekend depending on how you feel.

Serves 2

1 small butternut squash
1 bag of spinach
3 cloves of chopped garlic
2 tablespoons of pinenuts
1 teaspoon of oregano
½ teaspoon of sweet smoked paprika
2 handfuls of halved baby plum tomatoes
2 good heaps of parmesan

Pre-heat oven to 190°C.

Roast the whole butternut squash for up to an hour, until soft and juicy. Fry the garlic and pinenuts, and towards the end add the herbs, spices and tomatoes with the spinach to slightly wilt. Halve the squash, put on two plates, pour over the spinach mixture and cover with parmesan. This could be grilled to melt or eaten just as it is.

GARLIC FARM
WOOD PIGEON KIEVS

Another winner in The Garlic Farm Café. Charlie really knows about combining flavours of local ingredients and this shows both off brilliantly.

Serves 2

2 wood pigeon breasts, skinned and cut through the breast sideways on to make a pocket
1 leek washed and cut thinly
Small handful of dry toasted pine nuts
1/4 packet of butter
2 cloves of Purple Moldovan or Solent Wight Garlic
3 large IOW Maris Piper potatoes
Handful of baby leaf spinach
Knob of butter

1 egg and 100ml milk beaten together
1 tablespoon stone ground plain flour
3 tablespoons breadcrumbs mixed with salt, pepper and chopped thyme
Sweet tomato and herb chutney

Make garlic butter by crushing the garlic into softened butter and beating together. This can be kept in the fridge until needed and of course, any excess can be used for anything else you fancy. Dry pan fry the pine nuts until golden brown. Remove the pine nuts and, in the same pan, sweat the sliced leeks until tender, cool slightly and then mix together with the pine nuts and garlic butter. Using a teaspoon, place a spoonful of the butter and leek mixture into the pocket of the pigeon and use the small filet from the bottom of the breast to seal in the mixture. Roll in the seasoned flour, drop into the egg and milk mixture and then into the breadcrumb mixture. Be careful at this stage not to over-clog the pigeon with too many breadcrumbs, place on a plate and refrigerate for an hour.

Make mashed potato by peeling potatoes and placing

> "Charlie really knows about combining local flavours"

into salted water to cook; when tender, drain and mash with a little butter and seasoning. Whilst hot, add the washed spinach leaves and mix well - you can add a dash of quality extra virgin olive oil for that glossy look!

Deep fry the Pigeon Kievs for about 5-7 min at about 180°C, drain on absorbent paper and place on a plate with a heap of mash and a good dollop of our own sweet tomato and herb chutney.

Kievs can also be baked for 10 minutes at 220°C if you don't deep fry.

BRAISED SHOULDER OF PORK IN PRUNE JUICE

"plenty of flavour infused through the prune juice"

Great eaten hot or cold, lean and healthy and incredibly easy. The meat is succulent and sweet with plenty of flavour infused through the prune juice.

Shoulder of pork, boned and skin removed
1 carton of prune juice (or half carton prune juice plus 2-3 glasses red wine)
7-8 large garlic cloves
2 teaspoons of fennel seeds
2 teaspoons of cumin seeds
1 bay leaf
1 carrot, chopped
1 onion, finely sliced
1 celery stick, chopped

Put all of the ingredients into a large casserole, cover and cook in the oven at 150°C for 3 hours. You can prepare this the night before and leave in the fridge to marinate overnight before cooking. After 3 hours, remove from the oven, take out the pork and strain the liquid into a smaller pan. Reduce the liquid to a delicious, thick, syrup-like gravy. A great way to serve this dish is to slice the pork into a serving dish then pour the gravy back over the meat. It's perfect served with mash and spring greens.

CHUTNEYS AND RELISHES

Ideas for using Garlic Farm Chutneys and Relishes

Garlic, Apricot and Ginger Chutney

This is the original garlic farm chutney made by Jenny in the farmhouse kitchen about ten years ago and still a firm favourite. Apart from being excellent alongside a plate of cheeses or meats, we've also recommended this chutney to add to the Summer Barbecue Burger mix. Also try Charlie's trick of adding it to sausage meat for extra tasty sausage rolls.

Rhubarb and Pear Chutney

Columbine, our main recipe contributor, came up with the incredible combination of this chutney with baked mackerel. Amazing. You could also try it with ice cream... no, really.

Fig, Apple and Ginger Chutney

Some people just can't stay away from figs. Grandad Martin grows beautiful specimens in his garden so we've all grown up to be rather fond of them. Try this chutney with goat's cheese or with pigeon paté.

Garlic, Tomato and Ginger Chutney

This makes a brilliant addition to summer burgers but also great added to marinades for any kind of meat.

Cheeky Monkey (Banana)

This really isn't just a gimmick. Strangely, it works very well with cottage cheese and is also good with curries.

Peach and Mango

One of our favourite alternatives to traditional mango chutney with curries. Also great added to a dressing for a smoked mackerel salad.

Garlic Pic à l'Aili

What can one do with pic à l'aili apart from just marvel that anyone could come up with that name? Like the traditional version, a classic but more garlicky addition to any farmhouse ploughman's lunch.

Vampire's Delight (Sweet Apple)

Try using this to marinate pork chops, absolutely delicious. Or just use as a condiment with roast pork.

Vampire Relish (Spicy Tomato)

This stuff just vanishes in flash with tortilla crisps. Also try our very easy Garlic Farm guacamole by combining 2 mashed avocados with half a jar of Vampire Relish and juice of one lime.

GARLIC
TOMATO
& GINGER CHUTNEY

A Classic Tomato Chutney with
an elegant Garlic Bouquet.

INGREDIENTS
Chopped Tomatoes 38%,
Cider Vinegar, Brown Sugar, Apple,
Sultanas, Garlic 5%, Ginger 4%,
Onion, Mixed Spice, Salt

The Garlic Farm
070110

INGREDIENTS
Cider Vinegar, Cauliflower 18%,
White Sugar, Courgettes, Garlic 10%,
Carrots, Tomato, Celery, Onion,
Mustard, Turmeric

The Garlic Farm
251 209

! RIPE A
½ LEMON
I CLOVE
½ RED ON
I RIPE !

SOUR CRE

LAY TO
BAKING
OVEN OR
WHILST
USING A
REMOVE
ON TOP,
SERVE

Vampire Repent (Plum and Chilli)
Give your lamb chops a bit of a zing by marinating them
in this before roasting.

Pickled Garlic with Curry (Whole Garlic Cloves)
This is a favourite amongst the lads eaten on cocktail sticks with a beer.
Crunchy and delicious just by themselves. You could also add them whole to
any curry for a crunchy surprise.

Garlic and Onion Marmalade.
Perfect accompaniment to sausages and mash. Also great with cheddar
cheese or ham.

Sweet Tomato, Garlic & Herb Chutney
Add to salad, pasta sauces, sandwiches or barbecue foods. Also works well
as an ingredient. See our Hearty Lentil Pie recipe.

Condiments

Garlic and Creamed Horseradish
The obvious accompaniment to roast beef. Also great with smoked fish.

Toasted Garlic Mayonnaise
Use it in your BLT for extra flavour or on it's own as a dip with fat chips.

Garlic and Chilli Dijon Mustard
As with most mustards, great with sausages. Try tossing cocktail sausages in
this after cooking to give a delicious glaze.

Organic Garlic Mayonnaise
Another great sandwich treat or just to dunk your breadsticks in.

Sweet 'n' sour Chilli Sauce
Perfect for marinating ribs. Also a good addition to stir fry dishes.

Garlic and Horseradish Mustard
We use this with almost all cold meats. It's got such a great zing it livens
up any cold dish. Also a brilliant addition to salad dressings- see our salad
dressing recipes.

PICKLED GARLIC
WITH CURRY

Great with Ice Cold Beer
and a Poppadom.

GARLIC DRESSINGS

For all occasions

Classic Vinaigrette
(perfect accompaniment to a simple leaf salad)

2 teaspoons white wine vinegar
1/4 teaspoon sea salt
Freshly ground black pepper
½ teaspoon
Dijon mustard
1 clove garlic, peeled and minced
1/4 cup (60 ml) extra-virgin olive oil or sunflower oil for a lighter dressing

Garlic and coriander yoghurt dressing
(great with couscous salads and aubergines)

4 heaped tablespoons of Greek-style natural yogurt
2 teaspoons of lemon juice
1 fat garlic clove, crushed
A small knob ginger, finely chopped
A small handful coriander, roughly chopped

Moroccan dressing
(serve on beetroot and mixed vegetable or bean salads)

6 tablespoons extra-virgin olive oil
3 tablespoons red wine vinegar
1 teaspoon of sweet paprika
½ teaspoon of ground cumin
1 garlic clove, finely chopped
A small bunch of flat-leaf parsley, chopped,
save some leaves for decoration

Red pepper and garlic dressing
(serve hot with prawn or chicken salad)

1 tablespoon of olive oil
½ onion, finely chopped
1 garlic clove, chopped
1 red pepper, chopped
100ml white wine
½ teaspoon sea salt

Gently fry the onion and garlic in the oil until tender, add the peppers and white wine and boil for about 5 minutes until peppers are softened, season to taste.

Wendy's sundried tomato and garlic dressing
(stir through roast pumpkin & chickpeas, pasta or potatoes)

A few sundried tomatoes
5 tablespoons of red wine vinegar
3 cloves of garlic
1 tablespoon of balsamic vinegar
1 teaspoon sugar
Sea salt and freshly ground black pepper

Heat the vinegar and sundried tomatoes together and allow the tomatoes to soak in the hot vinegar to soften. Place all the ingredients in a food processor and whizz lightly. Do not over blend as it should remain slightly chunky.

GARLIC FOR HEALTH

The wonder plant

Garlic has been used for centuries as a remedy for a wide variety of ailments. The ancient Greeks, Romans, Japanese, Chinese and Egyptians were all believers in the healing powers of the stinking rose. Now, an increasing amount of scientific evidence suggests that these remedies are more than just folklore. It is no coincidence that garlic is listed amongst the top superfoods as it contains powerful antioxidants, antiseptic, antiviral and antifungal properties. Here are just some of the ways in which garlic can help keep you fit and healthy... and feeling sexy.

It is worth noting that in order to get the best medicinal benefits from your garlic, it should be eaten raw. It is only when the chemical components of the garlic are allowed to interact through crushing or chewing that the healing Allicin is released. If popping raw cloves in your mouth doesn't appeal, you can crush it into warm water (not boiling as this will kill the allicin) and mix with honey. Try chewing parsley afterwards to keep that garlic breath at bay.

Antiseptic properties

As an antiseptic, garlic acts in two ways, killing both bacteria and fungi. This means that it is useful in treating mild intestinal infections such as diarrhoea as well as lung infections such as bronchitis. It also seems to act as a protective agent against these infections if taken regularly.

Applying a topical solution of raw garlic and water may prevent infection. Simply crush one clove of garlic and mix it in one-third of a cup of clean water. Use the solution within three hours because it will lose its potency over time. A garlic solution used as a footbath several times a day is thought to improve athlete's foot.

Research has shown that a garlic oil extract cured all warts it was applied to within two weeks. In the same study, the garlic oil extract also proved useful in dissolving corns.

CAUTION: Always use a diluted garlic solution when applying garlic directly to the skin. Pure cut garlic is quite astringent so prolonged exposure to the skin may result in a burn.

Garlic and your gums
Research has concluded that garlic inhibits disease-causing bacteria in the mouth and may be valuable in fighting periodontitis, a serious gum disease.

A garlic gargle of crushed garlic in warm water can also help to heal mouth ulcers.

Cancer
Experiments in the laboratory and in population studies all support the premise that garlic may interfere with tumour activity. Cancers of the stomach, colon and skin seem to be the most likely to be affected. The exact mechanism is unclear and probably consists of several different actions but intake of fresh garlic definitely shows promising results.

What is certain is that garlic acts as a powerful antioxidant helping to protect against free radicals in the body, which are known to cause damage to cells and encourage cancers.

Natural insect repellent
When garlic is eaten and its components are metabolized, compounds are released from the body through the skin and breath, which can help ward off bugs.

Garlic has a long folk tradition as an insect pest repellent for use in the garden. Used as a spray of crushed garlic in water it can combat aphids, white flies, spiders and other pests. Garlic's insect repellent abilities are more than just folklore. Diallyl disulfide and diallyl trisulfide, two compounds in garlic oil, are insecticidal. In scientific studies, garlic has successfully destroyed mosquito larvae and certain species of ticks, and has repelled mosquitoes, black flies, fruit flies and fleas. Garlic cloves strategically placed in your fruit bowl will keep away the summer fruit flies.

Garlic has also demonstrated success repelling larger pests, including rabbits, moles and deer. It can be used to prevent the spread of mould and repel insects from stored fruit, and some people even place garlic in drawers to repel moths.

Cardiovascular health
Garlic's role in cardiovascular health cannot be underestimated. Numerous scientific studies have revealed garlic's potential as food for the heart. It may help to lower cholesterol, lower blood pressure, prevent platelet aggregation and thrombosis and contain powerful antioxidants; all important in maintaining a healthy cardiovascular system.

Norah and Martin Boswell – Garlic's magic at work?

Flu fighter

Taking three cloves a day when you have a cold may help you feel better. If the raw garlic bothers your stomach, take it minced and mixed with olive oil.

Herbalists recommend chewing garlic and holding it in your mouth for a while before swallowing it to obtain the best dose of bacteria-fighting allicin.

Other folk remedies

Battle colds and chest congestion with a garlic poultice or plaster. To make one, put some chopped garlic in a clean cloth, or paper towel. Fold it over to enclose the garlic. Pour very warm (but not hot) water over the wrapped garlic, let it sit for a few seconds, and then lightly wring it out. Place the wrapped garlic on the chest for several minutes. Reheat with very warm water and place on the back, over the lung area, for several minutes.

Garlic in the bedroom

Garlic is a time-honoured remedy in many ancient traditions for improving male sexual performance and has a strong reputation in some cultures as an aphrodisiac. In fact, there is some scientific proof for this as garlic improves blood flow... to all parts of the body.

Dr Joerg Gruenwald of Berlin University said: "A lot of men with heart disease will have impotence but not realise poor circulation and narrowing of the arteries in the groin is to blame. Garlic can help. A good flow of blood to the groin means a man should not have a problem with sex."

Not quite an aphrodisiac but possibly enough to account for garlic's unlikely romantic reputation? Roll over Viagra.

THE
GARLIC
FARM

ON THE ISLE OF WIGHT

SUPPORT BRITISH FARMERS

2010

E LADY FARMERS
ALENDAR

GARLIC FOLKLORE

By Alexa Boswell.

Of course, we've always known that garlic is all-powerful, magical and mysterious. It wards off evil spirits, fends against vampires and can even act as a vital ingredient in a love spell. Here are a few snippets of historical garlic superstition and myth from the Ancient Greeks to Bram Stoker.

The Europeans

Central European folk beliefs considered garlic a powerful ward against devils, werewolves, and vampires. To ward off vampires, garlic could be worn on one's person, hung in windows, or rubbed on chimneys and keyholes.

Legend has it that one can rid oneself of a lovesick former lover by sticking two crossed pins in a garlic bulb and placing it at a crossroads. Lure the lover until he crosses it, and he will lose interest.

Eating and carrying garlic is believed to enhance speed, strength, courage and endurance, and soldiers throughout history have used it for these properties when going into battle.

It is said that if you carry a garlic clove with you when travelling over water, it will prevent you from drowning.

Gypsy love spell

Upon a garlic bulb, write the name of the man or woman you wish to have as your lover. Plant the bulb in a red clay pot, in fertile soil with a drop of your blood. As you do this, repeat the name of your intended aloud.

Every day at sunset and sunrise you must
water the pot and recite these words:
"As this root grows, so shall the love of
(full name of man or woman) grow for me."

Vampires

In many vampire stories, garlic is used as an effective weapon against the bloodsucking creatures. Bram Stoker, the author of the most famous vampire story of all, is partly responsible for this concept and in 'Dracula' he makes several references to garlic. Here are some quotes from the novel:

"Lucy lay in her coffin, strewn with the wild garlic flowers, which sent through the odour of lily and rose, a heavy, overpowering smell into the night."

"I shall cut off her head and fill her mouth with garlic, and I shall drive a stake through her body."

"I had laid over the clamps of those doors garlic, which the Un-Dead cannot bear"

When diseases caused by mosquito bites were considered "The touch of the vampire," garlic came in handy as a mosquito repellent.

The Greeks

In Greece, athletes would take copious amounts of garlic before competition, and Greek soldiers would consume garlic before going into battle. It also became common in ancient Greece for midwives to hang garlic cloves in birthing rooms to keep the evil spirits at bay. Homer reported that Ulysses owed his escape from Circe to "yellow garlic".

The Egyptians

Egyptian slaves were given a daily ration of garlic, as it was believed to ward off illness and to increase strength and endurance.

During the reign of King Tutankhamen of Egypt, fifteen pounds of garlic would buy a healthy male slave.

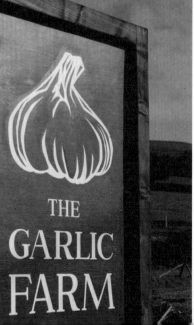

THE GARLIC FARM

PICKLED GARLIC WITH CURRY
Great with Ice Cold Beer and a Poppadom.